TEACHER'S PET PUBLICATIONS

PUZZLE PACK
for
The Miracle Worker

based on the book by
William Gibson

Written by
Mary B. Collins

© 2005 Teacher's Pet Publications
All Rights Reserved

The materials in this packet are copyrighted
by Teacher's Pet Publications, Inc.

These pages may be duplicated by the purchaser
for use in the purchaser's own classroom.

Copying any of these materials and distributing them
for any other purpose is a violation of the copyright laws.

© 2005 Teacher's Pet Publications, Inc.
www.tpet.com

INTRODUCTION
If you already own the LitPlan for this title, this Puzzle Pack will refresh your Unit Resource Materials and Vocabulary Resource Materials sections plus give you additional materials you can substitute into the tests. If you do not already have a complete LitPlan, these pages will give you some supplemental materials to use with your own plan. There are two main groups of materials: one set for unit words (such as characters' names, symbols, places, etc.) and one set for vocabulary words associated with the book.

WORD LIST
There is a word list for both the unit words and the vocabulary words. These lists show you which words are being used in the materials and the clues or definitions being used for those words. You may want to give students a word list with clues/definitions to help them, or you may want students to only have a word list (without clues/definitions) if you want them to work a little harder. Both are available for duplication. The word lists can also be your "calling key" for the bingo games.

FILL IN THE BLANK AND MATCHING
There are 4 each of the fill in the blank and matching worksheets for both the unit and vocabulary words. These pages can be used either as extra worksheets for students or as objective parts of a unit test. They can be done individually if students need extra help or as a whole class activity to review the material covered.

MAGIC SQUARES
The magic squares not only reinforce the material covered but also work on reasoning and math skills. Many teachers have told us that their students really enjoy doing these!

WORD SEARCH PUZZLES
The word search words go in all directions, as indicated on your answer keys. Two of the word search puzzles have the clues listed rather than the words. This makes the puzzle a little more difficult, but it reinforces the material better. Two word search puzzles have words only for students who find the clue puzzles too difficult.

CROSSWORD PUZZLES
Both unit and vocabulary word sections have 4 crossword puzzles.

BINGO CARDS
There are 32 individual bingo cards for the unit words and 32 individual bingo cards for the vocabulary words. You can use your word list as a "call list," calling the words at random and marking them off of your list as you go, or you could use the flash cards by cutting them apart and drawing the words at random from a hat (or box or whatever). To make a better review, you might ask for the definition and spelling of each word as you call it out–or you could call out the definitions and have students tell you the words they need to look for on the puzzle.

JUGGLE LETTERS
The vocabulary juggle letter game is intended to help students learn the spellings of the words. One sheet has the definitions listed on it as an extra help for students who need it or to reinforce the definitions if you choose to do so.

FLASH CARDS
We've included a set of vocabulary flash cards you can duplicate, cut, and fold for your students. Some teachers make a few sets for general use by the class; others make a set for each student. Some teachers duplicate them for each student and have the students cut & fold their own. You can cut out just the words and put them in a hat, have each student pick out one word and write the definition and a sentence for that word. Students then swap words and papers, with the next student adding a sentence of his own under the last one. You can have students swap as many times as you like. Each time the student will read the sentences written prior to his own and then add a sentence. You can cut out the words and definitions separately and play "I Have; Who Has?" Each student in the room draws a word and definition. The first student says, "I have (the name of the word). Who has the definition?" The student with the definition reads it then says, "I have (the name of the vocabulary word she has). Who has the definition?" The round continues until all words and definitions have been given.

Miracle Worker Unit Word List

No.	Word	Clue/Definition
1.	ANAGNOS	Annie's mentor from Perkins Institute
2.	ANGEL	Baby Martha
3.	ANNE	She has not loved a soul since her brother's death
4.	BELL	Used by Percy to alert family of Helen's outburst
5.	BITE	Helen does this to her fingers in her mouth
6.	BOSTON	Perkins Institute location
7.	BUTTONS	Torn off Aunt Ev's dress by Helen for doll's eyes
8.	CARRIAGE	Driven to pick up Annie at the train station
9.	CHEEK	A touch here means Kate
10.	CRAMP	Annie has this from signing to Helen: writer's ___
11.	CROCHET	Helen made a string of wool doing this craft
12.	DEADHOUSE	Asylum playroom for Annie and Jimmy
13.	DEVIL	Annie called Helen this after she hid the room key
14.	DICTIONARY	Used by Annie to spell correctly
15.	DOCTOR	Diagnoses baby Helen with acute congestion
16.	DOLLS	Martha and Percy play with paper ___
17.	EYELIDS	Doll blind girls give Annie for Helen has movable ___
18.	FOREVER	Promise of love to Jimmy and then Helen
19.	GARDEN	Home for Annie and Helen for two weeks: ___ house
20.	GIBSON	Playwright
21.	GIVING	Original sin according to Annie: ___ up
22.	GLASSES	Annie's trademark: smoked ___
23.	HELEN	Like a little safe, locked, that no one can open
24.	IVY	Keller estate in Alabama: ___ Green
25.	JAMES	Thinks half-sister Helen should be in asylum
26.	JIMMY	Haunting voice in Annie's mind
27.	KATE	A woman steeled in grief
28.	KELLER	Views women as the flowers of civilization: Captain ___
29.	KEY	Dropped by Helen into the well
30.	LADDER	Fetched by James to rescue Annie
31.	LANGUAGE	Is to the mind more than light is to the eye
32.	MARTHA	Helen's female Negro playmate
33.	MILDRED	Helen's younger sibling
34.	MOUSETRAP	Helen's mind worked like one
35.	NAPKIN	Folded by Helen
36.	NEEDLE	Used to jab Annie
37.	OBEDIENCE	Gateway through which knowledge enters the mind
38.	PAPA	Sign for Captain Keller
39.	PERCY	Helen puts her fingers in his mouth
40.	PERKINS	Institute for the blind in Boston
41.	PITCHER	Needed to be refilled at the pump
42.	PITY	Captain wishes Annie would show some
43.	RATS	Playthings for Annie and Jimmy in asylum
44.	RING	Going away present from Anagnos
45.	SCISSORS	Taken from Martha forcefully by Helen
46.	SULLIVAN	Anne's last name
47.	TEACHER	Sign for Annie
48.	TEWKSBURY	Institution where Jimmy died
49.	THREE	Number of acts in this play
50.	TOOTH	It was knocked out when Helen hit Annie with the doll
51.	TRAIN	How Annie traveled from Boston to Alabama
52.	TUSCUMBIA	Town in AL where Kellers reside
53.	TWENTY	Governess's age

Miracle Worker Unit Word List

No.	Word	Clue/Definition
54.	TWENTY-FIVE	Number of dollars a week Annie is paid
55.	VINEY	Negro servant
56.	WATER	Breakthrough word for Helen

Miracle Worker Fill In The Blank 1

_____ 1. Martha and Percy play with paper ___
_____ 2. Helen puts her fingers in his mouth
_____ 3. Asylum playroom for Annie and Jimmy
_____ 4. Is to the mind more than light is to the eye
_____ 5. How Annie traveled from Boston to Alabama
_____ 6. Used by Annie to spell correctly
_____ 7. Number of acts in this play
_____ 8. It was knocked out when Helen hit Annie with the doll
_____ 9. Helen's mind worked like one
_____ 10. Fetched by James to rescue Annie
_____ 11. Torn off Aunt Ev's dress by Helen for doll's eyes
_____ 12. Haunting voice in Annie's mind
_____ 13. Annie's mentor from Perkins Institute
_____ 14. Views women as the flowers of civilization: Captain ___
_____ 15. Helen's female Negro playmate
_____ 16. Captain wishes Annie would show some
_____ 17. Keller estate in Alabama: ___ Green
_____ 18. Breakthrough word for Helen
_____ 19. Thinks half-sister Helen should be in asylum
_____ 20. Like a little safe, locked, that no one can open

Miracle Worker Fill In The Blank 1 Answer Key

DOLLS	1. Martha and Percy play with paper ___
PERCY	2. Helen puts her fingers in his mouth
DEADHOUSE	3. Asylum playroom for Annie and Jimmy
LANGUAGE	4. Is to the mind more than light is to the eye
TRAIN	5. How Annie traveled from Boston to Alabama
DICTIONARY	6. Used by Annie to spell correctly
THREE	7. Number of acts in this play
TOOTH	8. It was knocked out when Helen hit Annie with the doll
MOUSETRAP	9. Helen's mind worked like one
LADDER	10. Fetched by James to rescue Annie
BUTTONS	11. Torn off Aunt Ev's dress by Helen for doll's eyes
JIMMY	12. Haunting voice in Annie's mind
ANAGNOS	13. Annie's mentor from Perkins Institute
KELLER	14. Views women as the flowers of civilization: Captain ___
MARTHA	15. Helen's female Negro playmate
PITY	16. Captain wishes Annie would show some
IVY	17. Keller estate in Alabama: ___ Green
WATER	18. Breakthrough word for Helen
JAMES	19. Thinks half-sister Helen should be in asylum
HELEN	20. Like a little safe, locked, that no one can open

Miracle Worker Fill In The Blank 2

_____ 1. Baby Martha
_____ 2. Original sin according to Annie: ___ up
_____ 3. Breakthrough word for Helen
_____ 4. It was knocked out when Helen hit Annie with the doll
_____ 5. How Annie traveled from Boston to Alabama
_____ 6. Town in AL where Kellers reside
_____ 7. Number of acts in this play
_____ 8. Helen's female Negro playmate
_____ 9. Diagnoses baby Helen with acute congestion
_____ 10. Martha and Percy play with paper ___
_____ 11. Views women as the flowers of civilization: Captain ___
_____ 12. Governess's age
_____ 13. Thinks half-sister Helen should be in asylum
_____ 14. Annie's mentor from Perkins Institute
_____ 15. Keller estate in Alabama: ___ Green
_____ 16. Sign for Annie
_____ 17. Fetched by James to rescue Annie
_____ 18. Home for Annie and Helen for two weeks: ___ house
_____ 19. Institute for the blind in Boston
_____ 20. Is to the mind more than light is to the eye

Miracle Worker Fill In The Blank 2 Answer Key

ANGEL	1. Baby Martha
GIVING	2. Original sin according to Annie: ___ up
WATER	3. Breakthrough word for Helen
TOOTH	4. It was knocked out when Helen hit Annie with the doll
TRAIN	5. How Annie traveled from Boston to Alabama
TUSCUMBIA	6. Town in AL where Kellers reside
THREE	7. Number of acts in this play
MARTHA	8. Helen's female Negro playmate
DOCTOR	9. Diagnoses baby Helen with acute congestion
DOLLS	10. Martha and Percy play with paper ___
KELLER	11. Views women as the flowers of civilization: Captain ___
TWENTY	12. Governess's age
JAMES	13. Thinks half-sister Helen should be in asylum
ANAGNOS	14. Annie's mentor from Perkins Institute
IVY	15. Keller estate in Alabama: ___ Green
TEACHER	16. Sign for Annie
LADDER	17. Fetched by James to rescue Annie
GARDEN	18. Home for Annie and Helen for two weeks: ___ house
PERKINS	19. Institute for the blind in Boston
LANGUAGE	20. Is to the mind more than light is to the eye

Miracle Worker Fill In The Blank 3

_____ 1. Keller estate in Alabama: ___ Green
_____ 2. Folded by Helen
_____ 3. Torn off Aunt Ev's dress by Helen for doll's eyes
_____ 4. Helen does this to her fingers in her mouth
_____ 5. Asylum playroom for Annie and Jimmy
_____ 6. Playwright
_____ 7. Needed to be refilled at the pump
_____ 8. It was knocked out when Helen hit Annie with the doll
_____ 9. Going away present from Anagnos
_____ 10. Baby Martha
_____ 11. Playthings for Annie and Jimmy in asylum
_____ 12. Annie's mentor from Perkins Institute
_____ 13. Thinks half-sister Helen should be in asylum
_____ 14. Haunting voice in Annie's mind
_____ 15. A touch here means Kate
_____ 16. Number of dollars a week Annie is paid
_____ 17. Institution where Jimmy died
_____ 18. Anne's last name
_____ 19. Martha and Percy play with paper ___
_____ 20. Number of acts in this play

Miracle Worker Fill In The Blank 3 Answer Key

IVY	1. Keller estate in Alabama: ___ Green
NAPKIN	2. Folded by Helen
BUTTONS	3. Torn off Aunt Ev's dress by Helen for doll's eyes
BITE	4. Helen does this to her fingers in her mouth
DEADHOUSE	5. Asylum playroom for Annie and Jimmy
GIBSON	6. Playwright
PITCHER	7. Needed to be refilled at the pump
TOOTH	8. It was knocked out when Helen hit Annie with the doll
RING	9. Going away present from Anagnos
ANGEL	10. Baby Martha
RATS	11. Playthings for Annie and Jimmy in asylum
ANAGNOS	12. Annie's mentor from Perkins Institute
JAMES	13. Thinks half-sister Helen should be in asylum
JIMMY	14. Haunting voice in Annie's mind
CHEEK	15. A touch here means Kate
TWENTY-FIVE	16. Number of dollars a week Annie is paid
TEWKSBURY	17. Institution where Jimmy died
SULLIVAN	18. Anne's last name
DOLLS	19. Martha and Percy play with paper ___
THREE	20. Number of acts in this play

Miracle Worker Fill In The Blank 4

_____ 1. Captain wishes Annie would show some
_____ 2. Fetched by James to rescue Annie
_____ 3. Dropped by Helen into the well
_____ 4. Used by Annie to spell correctly
_____ 5. Helen's younger sibling
_____ 6. Keller estate in Alabama: ___ Green
_____ 7. How Annie traveled from Boston to Alabama
_____ 8. Governess's age
_____ 9. Town in AL where Kellers reside
_____ 10. Original sin according to Annie: ___ up
_____ 11. Number of acts in this play
_____ 12. It was knocked out when Helen hit Annie with the doll
_____ 13. Doll blind girls give Annie for Helen has movable ___
_____ 14. Going away present fron Anagnos
_____ 15. Like a little safe, locked, that no one can open
_____ 16. Driven to pick up Annie at the train station
_____ 17. Annie has this from signing to Helen: writer's ___
_____ 18. Number of dollars a week Annie is paid
_____ 19. Anne's last name
_____ 20. Martha and Percy play with paper ___

Copyrighted

Miracle Worker Fill In The Blank 4 Answer Key

PITY	1. Captain wishes Annie would show some
LADDER	2. Fetched by James to rescue Annie
KEY	3. Dropped by Helen into the well
DICTIONARY	4. Used by Annie to spell correctly
MILDRED	5. Helen's younger sibling
IVY	6. Keller estate in Alabama: ___ Green
TRAIN	7. How Annie traveled from Boston to Alabama
TWENTY	8. Governess's age
TUSCUMBIA	9. Town in AL where Kellers reside
GIVING	10. Original sin according to Annie: ___ up
THREE	11. Number of acts in this play
TOOTH	12. It was knocked out when Helen hit Annie with the doll
EYELIDS	13. Doll blind girls give Annie for Helen has movable ___
RING	14. Going away present fron Anagnos
HELEN	15. Like a little safe, locked, that no one can open
CARRIAGE	16. Driven to pick up Annie at the train station
CRAMP	17. Annie has this from signing to Helen: writer's ___
TWENTY-FIVE	18. Number of dollars a week Annie is paid
SULLIVAN	19. Anne's last name
DOLLS	20. Martha and Percy play with paper ___

Miracle Worker Matching 1

___ 1. FOREVER   A. Gateway through which knowledge enters the mind
___ 2. OBEDIENCE   B. Number of dollars a week Annie is paid
___ 3. TEACHER   C. Town in AL where Kellers reside
___ 4. BOSTON   D. Breakthrough word for Helen
___ 5. NEEDLE   E. Helen does this to her fingers in her mouth
___ 6. SULLIVAN   F. Annie has this from signing to Helen: writer's ___
___ 7. TWENTY-FIVE   G. Negro servant
___ 8. SCISSORS   H. Helen made a string of wool doing this craft
___ 9. DEVIL   I. Doll blind girls give Annie for Helen has movable ___
___10. TWENTY   J. Governess's age
___11. BITE   K. Home for Annie and Helen for two weeks: ___ house
___12. VINEY   L. Thinks half-sister Helen should be in asylum
___13. TUSCUMBIA   M. Anne's last name
___14. WATER   N. Views women as the flowers of civilization: Captain ___
___15. EYELIDS   O. Used to jab Annie
___16. ANNE   P. Perkins Institute location
___17. CROCHET   Q. Promise of love to Jimmy and then Helen
___18. JAMES   R. Annie's mentor from Perkins Institute
___19. CRAMP   S. Sign for Annie
___20. KELLER   T. Used by Annie to spell correctly
___21. DICTIONARY   U. Taken from Martha forcefully by Helen
___22. BUTTONS   V. Annie called Helen this after she hid the room key
___23. GARDEN   W. She has not loved a soul since her brother's death
___24. ANAGNOS   X. Institute for the blind in Boston
___25. PERKINS   Y. Torn off Aunt Ev's dress by Helen for doll's eyes

Miracle Worker Matching 1 Answer Key

Q - 1.	FOREVER	A.	Gateway through which knowledge enters the mind
A - 2.	OBEDIENCE	B.	Number of dollars a week Annie is paid
S - 3.	TEACHER	C.	Town in AL where Kellers reside
P - 4.	BOSTON	D.	Breakthrough word for Helen
O - 5.	NEEDLE	E.	Helen does this to her fingers in her mouth
M - 6.	SULLIVAN	F.	Annie has this from signing to Helen: writer's ___
B - 7.	TWENTY-FIVE	G.	Negro servant
U - 8.	SCISSORS	H.	Helen made a string of wool doing this craft
V - 9.	DEVIL	I.	Doll blind girls give Annie for Helen has movable ___
J - 10.	TWENTY	J.	Governess's age
E - 11.	BITE	K.	Home for Annie and Helen for two weeks: ___ house
G - 12.	VINEY	L.	Thinks half-sister Helen should be in asylum
C - 13.	TUSCUMBIA	M.	Anne's last name
D - 14.	WATER	N.	Views women as the flowers of civilization: Captain ___
I - 15.	EYELIDS	O.	Used to jab Annie
W - 16.	ANNE	P.	Perkins Institute location
H - 17.	CROCHET	Q.	Promise of love to Jimmy and then Helen
L - 18.	JAMES	R.	Annie's mentor from Perkins Institute
F - 19.	CRAMP	S.	Sign for Annie
N - 20.	KELLER	T.	Used by Annie to spell correctly
T - 21.	DICTIONARY	U.	Taken from Martha forcefully by Helen
Y - 22.	BUTTONS	V.	Annie called Helen this after she hid the room key
K - 23.	GARDEN	W.	She has not loved a soul since her brother's death
R - 24.	ANAGNOS	X.	Institute for the blind in Boston
X - 25.	PERKINS	Y.	Torn off Aunt Ev's dress by Helen for doll's eyes

Miracle Worker Matching 2

___ 1. EYELIDS   A. Helen's younger sibling
___ 2. KELLER   B. Perkins Institute location
___ 3. ANAGNOS   C. Home for Annie and Helen for two weeks: ___ house
___ 4. DEADHOUSE   D. Sign for Annie
___ 5. TEACHER   E. Number of acts in this play
___ 6. HELEN   F. Folded by Helen
___ 7. ANGEL   G. Governess's age
___ 8. DOCTOR   H. Helen made a string of wool doing this craft
___ 9. BOSTON   I. How Annie traveled from Boston to Alabama
___10. GLASSES   J. It was knocked out when Helen hit Annie with the doll
___11. THREE   K. Helen does this to her fingers in her mouth
___12. PERKINS   L. Original sin according to Annie: ___ up
___13. LANGUAGE   M. Institute for the blind in Boston
___14. NAPKIN   N. Annie's mentor from Perkins Institute
___15. CROCHET   O. Annie's trademark: smoked ___
___16. TOOTH   P. Views women as the flowers of civilization: Captain ___
___17. TWENTY-FIVE Q. Diagnoses baby Helen with acute congestion
___18. TWENTY   R. Number of dollars a week Annie is paid
___19. GIVING   S. She has not loved a soul since her brother's death
___20. ANNE   T. Keller estate in Alabama: ___ Green
___21. TRAIN   U. Asylum playroom for Annie and Jimmy
___22. IVY   V. Baby Martha
___23. MILDRED   W. Like a little safe, locked, that no one can open
___24. BITE   X. Is to the mind more than light is to the eye
___25. GARDEN   Y. Doll blind girls give Annie for Helen has movable ___

Miracle Worker Matching 2 Answer Key

Y - 1.	EYELIDS	A.	Helen's younger sibling
P - 2.	KELLER	B.	Perkins Institute location
N - 3.	ANAGNOS	C.	Home for Annie and Helen for two weeks: ___ house
U - 4.	DEADHOUSE	D.	Sign for Annie
D - 5.	TEACHER	E.	Number of acts in this play
W - 6.	HELEN	F.	Folded by Helen
V - 7.	ANGEL	G.	Governess's age
Q - 8.	DOCTOR	H.	Helen made a string of wool doing this craft
B - 9.	BOSTON	I.	How Annie traveled from Boston to Alabama
O - 10.	GLASSES	J.	It was knocked out when Helen hit Annie with the doll
E - 11.	THREE	K.	Helen does this to her fingers in her mouth
M - 12.	PERKINS	L.	Original sin according to Annie: ___ up
X - 13.	LANGUAGE	M.	Institute for the blind in Boston
F - 14.	NAPKIN	N.	Annie's mentor from Perkins Institute
H - 15.	CROCHET	O.	Annie's trademark: smoked ___
J - 16.	TOOTH	P.	Views women as the flowers of civilization: Captain ___
R - 17.	TWENTY-FIVE	Q.	Diagnoses baby Helen with acute congestion
G - 18.	TWENTY	R.	Number of dollars a week Annie is paid
L - 19.	GIVING	S.	She has not loved a soul since her brother's death
S - 20.	ANNE	T.	Keller estate in Alabama: ___ Green
I - 21.	TRAIN	U.	Asylum playroom for Annie and Jimmy
T - 22.	IVY	V.	Baby Martha
A - 23.	MILDRED	W.	Like a little safe, locked, that no one can open
K - 24.	BITE	X.	Is to the mind more than light is to the eye
C - 25.	GARDEN	Y.	Doll blind girls give Annie for Helen has movable ___

Miracle Worker Matching 3

___ 1. BOSTON   A. Folded by Helen
___ 2. ANAGNOS   B. Gateway through which knowledge enters the mind
___ 3. OBEDIENCE   C. Sign for Captain Keller
___ 4. CRAMP   D. Fetched by James to rescue Annie
___ 5. JAMES   E. Helen made a string of wool doing this craft
___ 6. THREE   F. Playthings for Annie and Jimmy in asylum
___ 7. DICTIONARY   G. Annie has this from signing to Helen: writer's ___
___ 8. JIMMY   H. Used by Annie to spell correctly
___ 9. KELLER   I. Dropped by Helen into the well
___10. BELL   J. Helen's mind worked like one
___11. NAPKIN   K. Number of acts in this play
___12. LANGUAGE   L. Perkins Institute location
___13. MOUSETRAP   M. Thinks half-sister Helen should be in asylum
___14. CROCHET   N. Anne's last name
___15. EYELIDS   O. Needed to be refilled at the pump
___16. CHEEK   P. Annie's mentor from Perkins Institute
___17. PITY   Q. Helen does this to her fingers in her mouth
___18. SULLIVAN   R. Haunting voice in Annie's mind
___19. FOREVER   S. A touch here means Kate
___20. PAPA   T. Captain wishes Annie would show some
___21. KEY   U. Is to the mind more than light is to the eye
___22. PITCHER   V. Promise of love to Jimmy and then Helen
___23. RATS   W. Views women as the flowers of civilization: Captain ___
___24. BITE   X. Used by Percy to alert family of Helen's outburst
___25. LADDER   Y. Doll blind girls give Annie for Helen has movable ___

Miracle Worker Matching 3 Answer Key

L - 1.	BOSTON	A. Folded by Helen
P - 2.	ANAGNOS	B. Gateway through which knowledge enters the mind
B - 3.	OBEDIENCE	C. Sign for Captain Keller
G - 4.	CRAMP	D. Fetched by James to rescue Annie
M - 5.	JAMES	E. Helen made a string of wool doing this craft
K - 6.	THREE	F. Playthings for Annie and Jimmy in asylum
H - 7.	DICTIONARY	G. Annie has this from signing to Helen: writer's ___
R - 8.	JIMMY	H. Used by Annie to spell correctly
W - 9.	KELLER	I. Dropped by Helen into the well
X - 10.	BELL	J. Helen's mind worked like one
A - 11.	NAPKIN	K. Number of acts in this play
U - 12.	LANGUAGE	L. Perkins Institute location
J - 13.	MOUSETRAP	M. Thinks half-sister Helen should be in asylum
E - 14.	CROCHET	N. Anne's last name
Y - 15.	EYELIDS	O. Needed to be refilled at the pump
S - 16.	CHEEK	P. Annie's mentor from Perkins Institute
T - 17.	PITY	Q. Helen does this to her fingers in her mouth
N - 18.	SULLIVAN	R. Haunting voice in Annie's mind
V - 19.	FOREVER	S. A touch here means Kate
C - 20.	PAPA	T. Captain wishes Annie would show some
I - 21.	KEY	U. Is to the mind more than light is to the eye
O - 22.	PITCHER	V. Promise of love to Jimmy and then Helen
F - 23.	RATS	W. Views women as the flowers of civilization: Captain ___
Q - 24.	BITE	X. Used by Percy to alert family of Helen's outburst
D - 25.	LADDER	Y. Doll blind girls give Annie for Helen has movable ___

Miracle Worker Matching 4

___ 1. KEY   A. Martha and Percy play with paper ___
___ 2. MARTHA   B. How Annie traveled from Boston to Alabama
___ 3. FOREVER   C. Sign for Annie
___ 4. ANAGNOS   D. Used to jab Annie
___ 5. PITCHER   E. A woman steeled in grief
___ 6. OBEDIENCE   F. Anne's last name
___ 7. KATE   G. Fetched by James to rescue Annie
___ 8. CROCHET   H. Original sin according to Annie: ___ up
___ 9. DEADHOUSE   I. Gateway through which knowledge enters the mind
___10. TRAIN   J. A touch here means Kate
___11. GIVING   K. Helen's female Negro playmate
___12. NEEDLE   L. Taken from Martha forcefully by Helen
___13. TWENTY   M. Governess's age
___14. PERCY   N. Dropped by Helen into the well
___15. CRAMP   O. Asylum playroom for Annie and Jimmy
___16. ANNE   P. Torn off Aunt Ev's dress by Helen for doll's eyes
___17. SULLIVAN   Q. Thinks half-sister Helen should be in asylum
___18. WATER   R. Breakthrough word for Helen
___19. SCISSORS   S. Needed to be refilled at the pump
___20. DOLLS   T. Promise of love to Jimmy and then Helen
___21. BUTTONS   U. Annie has this from signing to Helen: writer's ___
___22. TEACHER   V. Helen puts her fingers in his mouth
___23. LADDER   W. She has not loved a soul since her brother's death
___24. JAMES   X. Annie's mentor from Perkins Institute
___25. CHEEK   Y. Helen made a string of wool doing this craft

Miracle Worker Matching 4 Answer Key

N - 1.	KEY	A. Martha and Percy play with paper ___
K - 2.	MARTHA	B. How Annie traveled from Boston to Alabama
T - 3.	FOREVER	C. Sign for Annie
X - 4.	ANAGNOS	D. Used to jab Annie
S - 5.	PITCHER	E. A woman steeled in grief
I - 6.	OBEDIENCE	F. Anne's last name
E - 7.	KATE	G. Fetched by James to rescue Annie
Y - 8.	CROCHET	H. Original sin according to Annie: ___ up
O - 9.	DEADHOUSE	I. Gateway through which knowledge enters the mind
B - 10.	TRAIN	J. A touch here means Kate
H - 11.	GIVING	K. Helen's female Negro playmate
D - 12.	NEEDLE	L. Taken from Martha forcefully by Helen
M - 13.	TWENTY	M. Governess's age
V - 14.	PERCY	N. Dropped by Helen into the well
U - 15.	CRAMP	O. Asylum playroom for Annie and Jimmy
W - 16.	ANNE	P. Torn off Aunt Ev's dress by Helen for doll's eyes
F - 17.	SULLIVAN	Q. Thinks half-sister Helen should be in asylum
R - 18.	WATER	R. Breakthrough word for Helen
L - 19.	SCISSORS	S. Needed to be refilled at the pump
A - 20.	DOLLS	T. Promise of love to Jimmy and then Helen
P - 21.	BUTTONS	U. Annie has this from signing to Helen: writer's ___
C - 22.	TEACHER	V. Helen puts her fingers in his mouth
G - 23.	LADDER	W. She has not loved a soul since her brother's death
Q - 24.	JAMES	X. Annie's mentor from Perkins Institute
J - 25.	CHEEK	Y. Helen made a string of wool doing this craft

Miracle Worker Magic Squares 1

Match the definition with the vocabulary word. Put your answers in the magic squares below. When your answers are correct, all columns and rows will add to the same number.

A. DOLLS
B. LANGUAGE
C. TEACHER
D. PITCHER
E. MARTHA
F. RATS
G. RING
H. OBEDIENCE
I. IVY
J. WATER
K. PITY
L. TOOTH
M. TUSCUMBIA
N. NEEDLE
O. BOSTON
P. TRAIN

1. Gateway through which knowledge enters the mind
2. Martha and Percy play with paper ___
3. Is to the mind more than light is to the eye
4. Going away present from Anagnos
5. Breakthrough word for Helen
6. Perkins Institute location
7. How Annie traveled from Boston to Alabama
8. Keller estate in Alabama: ___ Green
9. Captain wishes Annie would show some
10. Used to jab Annie
11. Town in AL where Kellers reside
12. It was knocked out when Helen hit Annie with the doll
13. Helen's female Negro playmate
14. Needed to be refilled at the pump
15. Sign for Annie
16. Playthings for Annie and Jimmy in asylum

A=	B=	C=	D=
E=	F=	G=	H=
I=	J=	K=	L=
M=	N=	O=	P=

Miracle Worker Magic Squares 1 Answer Key

Match the definition with the vocabulary word. Put your answers in the magic squares below. When your answers are correct, all columns and rows will add to the same number.

A. DOLLS
B. LANGUAGE
C. TEACHER
D. PITCHER
E. MARTHA
F. RATS
G. RING
H. OBEDIENCE
I. IVY
J. WATER
K. PITY
L. TOOTH
M. TUSCUMBIA
N. NEEDLE
O. BOSTON
P. TRAIN

1. Gateway through which knowledge enters the mind
2. Martha and Percy play with paper ___
3. Is to the mind more than light is to the eye
4. Going away present from Anagnos
5. Breakthrough word for Helen
6. Perkins Institute location
7. How Annie traveled from Boston to Alabama
8. Keller estate in Alabama: ___ Green
9. Captain wishes Annie would show some
10. Used to jab Annie
11. Town in AL where Kellers reside
12. It was knocked out when Helen hit Annie with the doll
13. Helen's female Negro playmate
14. Needed to be refilled at the pump
15. Sign for Annie
16. Playthings for Annie and Jimmy in asylum

A=2	B=3	C=15	D=14
E=13	F=16	G=4	H=1
I=8	J=5	K=9	L=12
M=11	N=10	O=6	P=7

Miracle Worker Magic Squares 2

Match the definition with the vocabulary word. Put your answers in the magic squares below. When your answers are correct, all columns and rows will add to the same number.

A. BITE
B. NEEDLE
C. LANGUAGE
D. DICTIONARY
E. PERCY
F. VINEY
G. TRAIN
H. THREE
I. CHEEK
J. CARRIAGE
K. CROCHET
L. GARDEN
M. ANNE
N. CRAMP
O. JIMMY
P. MILDRED

1. Used to jab Annie
2. How Annie traveled from Boston to Alabama
3. Helen made a string of wool doing this craft
4. Annie has this from signing to Helen: writer's ___
5. She has not loved a soul since her brother's death
6. Home for Annie and Helen for two weeks: ___ house
7. Number of acts in this play
8. Helen does this to her fingers in her mouth
9. Helen's younger sibling
10. A touch here means Kate
11. Helen puts her fingers in his mouth
12. Used by Annie to spell correctly
13. Is to the mind more than light is to the eye
14. Negro servant
15. Driven to pick up Annie at the train station
16. Haunting voice in Annie's mind

A=	B=	C=	D=
E=	F=	G=	H=
I=	J=	K=	L=
M=	N=	O=	P=

Miracle Worker Magic Squares 2 Answer Key

Match the definition with the vocabulary word. Put your answers in the magic squares below. When your answers are correct, all columns and rows will add to the same number.

A. BITE
B. NEEDLE
C. LANGUAGE
D. DICTIONARY
E. PERCY
F. VINEY
G. TRAIN
H. THREE
I. CHEEK
J. CARRIAGE
K. CROCHET
L. GARDEN
M. ANNE
N. CRAMP
O. JIMMY
P. MILDRED

1. Used to jab Annie
2. How Annie traveled from Boston to Alabama
3. Helen made a string of wool doing this craft
4. Annie has this from signing to Helen: writer's ___
5. She has not loved a soul since her brother's death
6. Home for Annie and Helen for two weeks: ___ house
7. Number of acts in this play
8. Helen does this to her fingers in her mouth
9. Helen's younger sibling
10. A touch here means Kate
11. Helen puts her fingers in his mouth
12. Used by Annie to spell correctly
13. Is to the mind more than light is to the eye
14. Negro servant
15. Driven to pick up Annie at the train station
16. Haunting voice in Annie's mind

A=8	B=1	C=13	D=12
E=11	F=14	G=2	H=7
I=10	J=15	K=3	L=6
M=5	N=4	O=16	P=9

Miracle Worker Magic Squares 3

Match the definition with the vocabulary word. Put your answers in the magic squares below. When your answers are correct, all columns and rows will add to the same number.

A. TWENTY   E. TWENTY-FIVE   I. OBEDIENCE   M. EYELIDS
B. CHEEK   F. ANNE   J. ANAGNOS   N. SULLIVAN
C. WATER   G. PERCY   K. GARDEN   O. PITCHER
D. MOUSETRAP   H. TEACHER   L. DEADHOUSE   P. LANGUAGE

1. She has not loved a soul since her brother's death
2. Gateway through which knowledge enters the mind
3. Needed to be refilled at the pump
4. Helen's mind worked like one
5. Doll blind girls give Annie for Helen has movable ___
6. A touch here means Kate
7. Sign for Annie
8. Home for Annie and Helen for two weeks: ___ house
9. Breakthrough word for Helen
10. Is to the mind more than light is to the eye
11. Annie's mentor from Perkins Institute
12. Number of dollars a week Annie is paid
13. Asylum playroom for Annie and Jimmy
14. Helen puts her fingers in his mouth
15. Governess's age
16. Anne's last name

A=	B=	C=	D=
E=	F=	G=	H=
I=	J=	K=	L=
M=	N=	O=	P=

Miracle Worker Magic Squares 3 Answer Key

Match the definition with the vocabulary word. Put your answers in the magic squares below. When your answers are correct, all columns and rows will add to the same number.

A. TWENTY
B. CHEEK
C. WATER
D. MOUSETRAP
E. TWENTY-FIVE
F. ANNE
G. PERCY
H. TEACHER
I. OBEDIENCE
J. ANAGNOS
K. GARDEN
L. DEADHOUSE
M. EYELIDS
N. SULLIVAN
O. PITCHER
P. LANGUAGE

1. She has not loved a soul since her brother's death
2. Gateway through which knowledge enters the mind
3. Needed to be refilled at the pump
4. Helen's mind worked like one
5. Doll blind girls give Annie for Helen has movable ___
6. A touch here means Kate
7. Sign for Annie
8. Home for Annie and Helen for two weeks: ___ house
9. Breakthrough word for Helen
10. Is to the mind more than light is to the eye
11. Annie's mentor from Perkins Institute
12. Number of dollars a week Annie is paid
13. Asylum playroom for Annie and Jimmy
14. Helen puts her fingers in his mouth
15. Governess's age
16. Anne's last name

A=15	B=6	C=9	D=4
E=12	F=1	G=14	H=7
I=2	J=11	K=8	L=13
M=5	N=16	O=3	P=10

Miracle Worker Magic Squares 4

Match the definition with the vocabulary word. Put your answers in the magic squares below. When your answers are correct, all columns and rows will add to the same number.

A. TUSCUMBIA E. TWENTY   I. TOOTH   M. THREE
B. RING   F. TEACHER   J. BUTTONS   N. CARRIAGE
C. HELEN   G. DICTIONARY K. MOUSETRAP O. SULLIVAN
D. GLASSES   H. CHEEK   L. PITCHER   P. NEEDLE

1. Anne's last name
2. Torn off Aunt Ev's dress by Helen for doll's eyes
3. A touch here means Kate
4. Town in AL where Kellers reside
5. Annie's trademark: smoked ___
6. Governess's age
7. Helen's mind worked like one
8. Driven to pick up Annie at the train station
9. Sign for Annie
10. Like a little safe, locked, that no one can open
11. Number of acts in this play
12. Needed to be refilled at the pump
13. It was knocked out when Helen hit Annie with the doll
14. Used to jab Annie
15. Going away present from Anagnos
16. Used by Annie to spell correctly

A=	B=	C=	D=
E=	F=	G=	H=
I=	J=	K=	L=
M=	N=	O=	P=

Miracle Worker Magic Squares 4 Answer Key

Match the definition with the vocabulary word. Put your answers in the magic squares below. When your answers are correct, all columns and rows will add to the same number.

A. TUSCUMBIA E. TWENTY   I. TOOTH   M. THREE
B. RING   F. TEACHER   J. BUTTONS   N. CARRIAGE
C. HELEN   G. DICTIONARY K. MOUSETRAP   O. SULLIVAN
D. GLASSES   H. CHEEK   L. PITCHER   P. NEEDLE

1. Anne's last name
2. Torn off Aunt Ev's dress by Helen for doll's eyes
3. A touch here means Kate
4. Town in AL where Kellers reside
5. Annie's trademark: smoked ___
6. Governess's age
7. Helen's mind worked like one
8. Driven to pick up Annie at the train station
9. Sign for Annie
10. Like a little safe, locked, that no one can open
11. Number of acts in this play
12. Needed to be refilled at the pump
13. It was knocked out when Helen hit Annie with the doll
14. Used to jab Annie
15. Going away present from Anagnos
16. Used by Annie to spell correctly

A=4	B=15	C=10	D=5
E=6	F=9	G=16	H=3
I=13	J=2	K=7	L=12
M=11	N=8	O=1	P=14

Miracle Worker Word Search 1

```
M D C A R R I A G E Z F W F K L L Z
C O T D R A W Y I Y K E L L E R A N
Y C R E P R E S V C H E E K Y J D T
L T R A A E E I I Z T Y G E P O D N
P O P A B C R Q N P E R N Y L J E X
N R N L M H H K G L S I A L M I R S
E N N X T P T E I T V I S I G M E Y
E K W O R N R D R N B X L Q N M H K
D A O P E T S L O M S D C W A Y C P
L T L D T F S E U B R G K J R S T B
E E R D I D G C S E E S L U B R I V
B A R D B A S X D W N D B A E O P G
G E Q F U U H G K D I S I T S S T N
R G L G T H K E E X K R A E P S N C
Z I N L Q X Z V L W P W D B N I E J
D A N O S B I G E E A R A T S C T S
L D B G N L X T W E N T Y D C S E Y
```

A touch here means Kate (5)
A woman steeled in grief (4)
Annie called Helen this after she hid the room key (5)
Annie has this from signing to Helen: writer's ___ (5)
Annie's trademark: smoked ___ (7)
Baby Martha (5)
Breakthrough word for Helen (5)
Captain wishes Annie would show some (4)
Diagnoses baby Helen with acute congestion (6)
Doll blind girls give Annie for Helen has movable ___ (7)
Driven to pick up Annie at the train station (8)
Dropped by Helen into the well (3)
Fetched by James to rescue Annie (6)
Folded by Helen (6)
Gateway through which knowledge enters the mind (9)
Going away present from Anagnos (4)
Governess's age (6)
Haunting voice in Annie's mind (5)
Helen does this to her fingers in her mouth (4)
Helen puts her fingers in his mouth (5)
Helen's younger sibling (7)
Home for Annie and Helen for two weeks: ___ house (6)
How Annie traveled from Boston to Alabama (5)
Institute for the blind in Boston (7)
Institution where Jimmy died (9)
Is to the mind more than light is to the eye (8)
It was knocked out when Helen hit Annie with the doll (5)
Keller estate in Alabama: ___ Green (3)
Like a little safe, locked, that no one can open (5)
Martha and Percy play with paper ___ (5)
Needed to be refilled at the pump (7)
Negro servant (5)
Number of acts in this play (5)
Original sin according to Annie: ___ up (6)
Playthings for Annie and Jimmy in asylum (4)
Playwright (6)
She has not loved a soul since her brother's death (4)
Sign for Annie (7)
Sign for Captain Keller (4)
Taken from Martha forcefully by Helen (8)
Thinks half-sister Helen should be in asylum (5)
Town in AL where Kellers reside (9)
Used by Percy to alert family of Helen's outburst (4)
Used to jab Annie (6)
Views women as the flowers of civilization: Captain ___ (6)

Miracle Worker Word Search 1 Answer Key

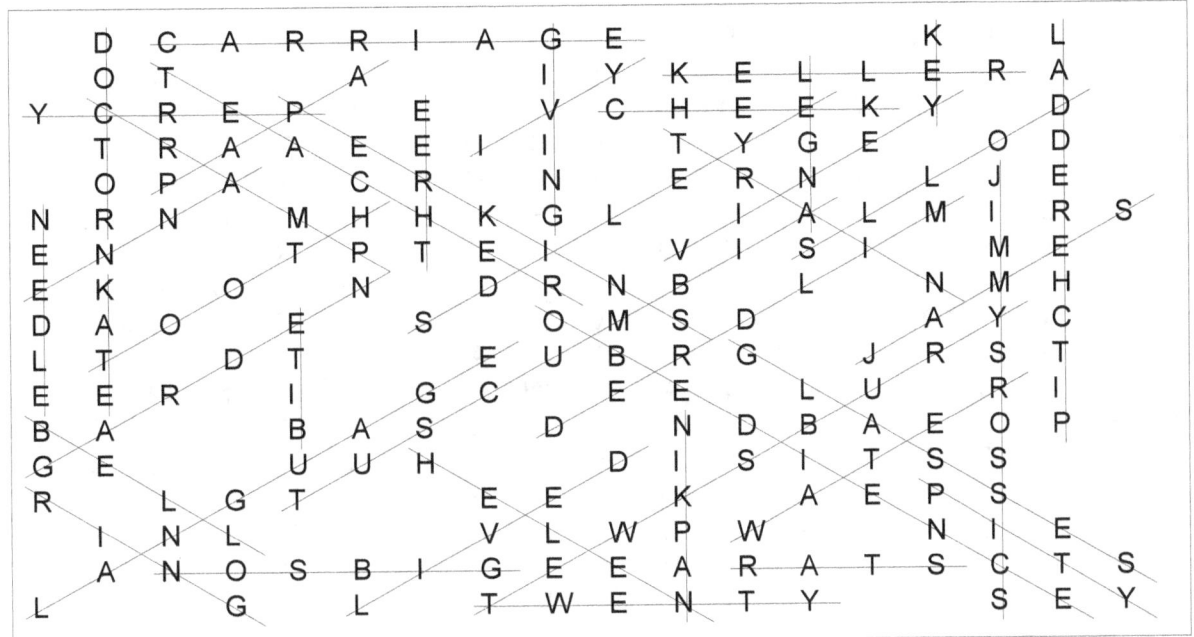

- A touch here means Kate (5)
- A woman steeled in grief (4)
- Annie called Helen this after she hid the room key (5)
- Annie has this from signing to Helen: writer's ___ (5)
- Annie's trademark: smoked ___ (7)
- Baby Martha (5)
- Breakthrough word for Helen (5)
- Captain wishes Annie would show some (4)
- Diagnoses baby Helen with acute congestion (6)
- Doll blind girls give Annie for Helen has movable ___ (7)
- Driven to pick up Annie at the train station (8)
- Dropped by Helen into the well (3)
- Fetched by James to rescue Annie (6)
- Folded by Helen (6)
- Gateway through which knowledge enters the mind (9)
- Going away present from Anagnos (4)
- Governess's age (6)
- Haunting voice in Annie's mind (5)
- Helen does this to her fingers in her mouth (4)
- Helen puts her fingers in his mouth (5)
- Helen's younger sibling (7)
- Home for Annie and Helen for two weeks: ___ house (6)
- How Annie traveled from Boston to Alabama (5)
- Institute for the blind in Boston (7)
- Institution where Jimmy died (9)
- Is to the mind more than light is to the eye (8)
- It was knocked out when Helen hit Annie with the doll (5)
- Keller estate in Alabama: ___ Green (3)
- Like a little safe, locked, that no one can open (5)
- Martha and Percy play with paper ___ (5)
- Needed to be refilled at the pump (7)
- Negro servant (5)
- Number of acts in this play (5)
- Original sin according to Annie: ___ up (6)
- Playthings for Annie and Jimmy in asylum (4)
- Playwright (6)
- She has not loved a soul since her brother's death (4)
- Sign for Annie (7)
- Sign for Captain Keller (4)
- Taken from Martha forcefully by Helen (8)
- Thinks half-sister Helen should be in asylum (5)
- Town in AL where Kellers reside (9)
- Used by Percy to alert family of Helen's outburst (4)
- Used to jab Annie (6)
- Views women as the flowers of civilization: Captain ___ (6)

Miracle Worker Word Search 2

```
T R A N X C L T E D G J I M M Y N R
E S N A Z J R L E N L S D I L E Y E
W W A P Q T D O I A L V L S L S T W
K F G K K E L V C S C D P N T B O D
S E N I E T I K F H R H F I P E O L
B S O N H G T E R E E X E K E B T K
U U S V I N E Y D O C T O R R O H Z
R O S E S S A L G H R X H E C S D C
Y H X E X D R T E A L T T P Y T M Y
G D M T X E Y E I G P A S K K O T F
R A T S D V K N A Y W H H C A N P F
J E R D I I A H W N Z E G K E T K Z
Z D A D G L T N D F N L C W R L E V
G L D F E R P V G O Q E T P K L L V
R I N G A N R A Q E L N B I T E L X
Z W P M A R C D P K L L Q T W B E G
O B E D I E N C E A V Z S Y H Q R L
```

A touch here means Kate (5)
A woman steeled in grief (4)
Annie called Helen this after she hid the room key (5)
Annie has this from signing to Helen: writer's ___ (5)
Annie's mentor from Perkins Institute (7)
Annie's trademark: smoked ___ (7)
Asylum playroom for Annie and Jimmy (9)
Baby Martha (5)
Breakthrough word for Helen (5)
Captain wishes Annie would show some (4)
Diagnoses baby Helen with acute congestion (6)
Doll blind girls give Annie for Helen has movable ___ (7)
Dropped by Helen into the well (3)
Fetched by James to rescue Annie (6)
Folded by Helen (6)
Gateway through which knowledge enters the mind (9)
Going away present from Anagnos (4)
Governess's age (6)
Haunting voice in Annie's mind (5)
Helen does this to her fingers in her mouth (4)
Helen made a string of wool doing this craft (7)
Helen puts her fingers in his mouth (5)
Helen's female Negro playmate (6)
Helen's younger sibling (7)
Home for Annie and Helen for two weeks: ___ house (6)
How Annie traveled from Boston to Alabama (5)
Institute for the blind in Boston (7)
Institution where Jimmy died (9)
It was knocked out when Helen hit Annie with the doll (5)
Keller estate in Alabama: ___ Green (3)
Like a little safe, locked, that no one can open (5)
Martha and Percy play with paper ___ (5)
Negro servant (5)
Number of acts in this play (5)
Original sin according to Annie: ___ up (6)
Perkins Institute location (6)
Playthings for Annie and Jimmy in asylum (4)
She has not loved a soul since her brother's death (4)
Sign for Annie (7)
Sign for Captain Keller (4)
Thinks half-sister Helen should be in asylum (5)
Used by Percy to alert family of Helen's outburst (4)
Used to jab Annie (6)
Views women as the flowers of civilization: Captain ___ (6)

Miracle Worker Word Search 2 Answer Key

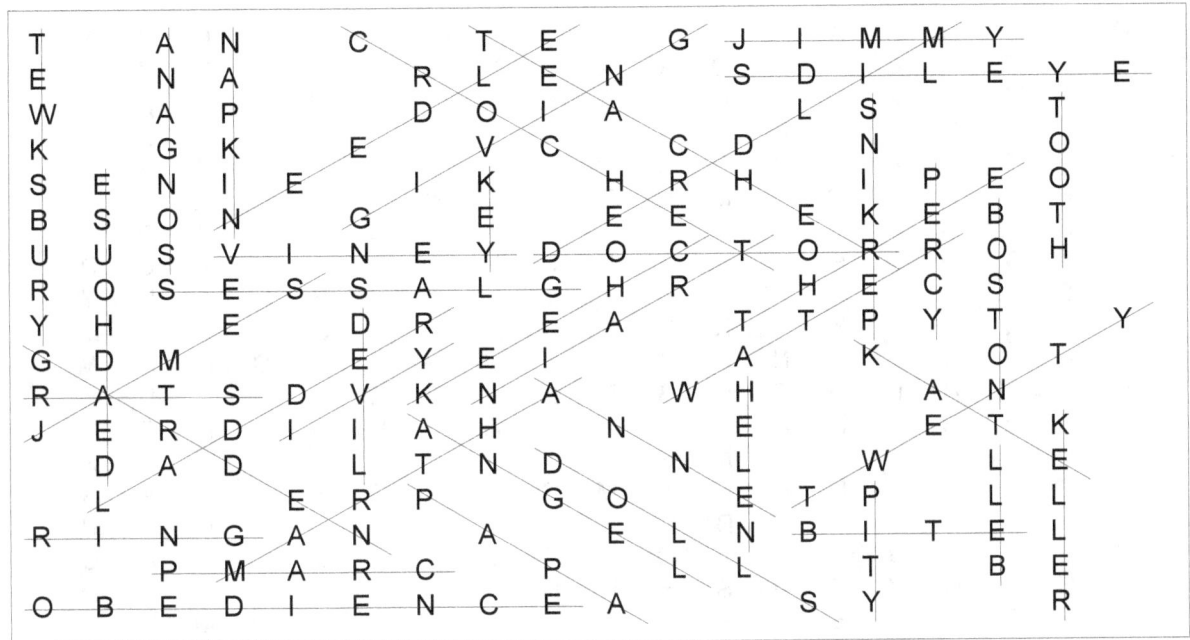

A touch here means Kate (5)
A woman steeled in grief (4)
Annie called Helen this after she hid the room key (5)
Annie has this from signing to Helen: writer's ___ (5)
Annie's mentor from Perkins Institute (7)
Annie's trademark: smoked ___ (7)
Asylum playroom for Annie and Jimmy (9)
Baby Martha (5)
Breakthrough word for Helen (5)
Captain wishes Annie would show some (4)
Diagnoses baby Helen with acute congestion (6)
Doll blind girls give Annie for Helen has movable ___ (7)
Dropped by Helen into the well (3)
Fetched by James to rescue Annie (6)
Folded by Helen (6)
Gateway through which knowledge enters the mind (9)
Going away present from Anagnos (4)
Governess's age (6)
Haunting voice in Annie's mind (5)
Helen does this to her fingers in her mouth (4)
Helen made a string of wool doing this craft (7)
Helen puts her fingers in his mouth (5)
Helen's female Negro playmate (6)

Helen's younger sibling (7)
Home for Annie and Helen for two weeks: ___ house (6)
How Annie traveled from Boston to Alabama (5)
Institute for the blind in Boston (7)
Institution where Jimmy died (9)
It was knocked out when Helen hit Annie with the doll (5)
Keller estate in Alabama: ___ Green (3)
Like a little safe, locked, that no one can open (5)
Martha and Percy play with paper ___ (5)
Negro servant (5)
Number of acts in this play (5)
Original sin according to Annie: ___ up (6)
Perkins Institute location (6)
Playthings for Annie and Jimmy in asylum (4)
She has not loved a soul since her brother's death (4)
Sign for Annie (7)
Sign for Captain Keller (4)
Thinks half-sister Helen should be in asylum (5)
Used by Percy to alert family of Helen's outburst (4)
Used to jab Annie (6)
Views women as the flowers of civilization: Captain ___ (6)

Miracle Worker Word Search 3

```
G C A R R I A G E G Q R K P T T J E B N
L M H D I C T I O N A R Y E D H C N Z K
A K T S S X M S L S A H N R L N R K L W
S Y R W Y U S Q J V K Q Y K E L R E P N
S P A P E F L Y S R O S S I C S E B E B
E W M L N G L M M B Y D N W L N R Q J
S W A I C F T F I B J E K S D F I K R V
C P A T D D R Y L V B F H E E M V V Q R
K R E V E R O F D O A J E T Y B I T E Y
T X O V A R Z A R S P N A M V J Y H G Y
P H I C D T X N E Z A K M M I L C N A M
I L T H H D W G D B P I T P E A R A U Z
T D E E O E F E G L J G R I E S E P G Y
C J W L Q T L N S A T P T K B P K N F
H H K E S Y H P L T M D U Y T E K I A S
E F S N E N Z Y B F Y O D S P L D N L R
R D B V E B O S T O N F U E C L R I N G
R W U D N Y T D S B N D I S R U B A R D
T N R T N P E O P Z Z S O V E C M M T D
N A Y C A Z N L G T D N N C E T H B M S
G I V I N G C G I B S O N X T O R E I C
F Q J Z A S R Y Q D S T L T W O N A E A
W H S N C V A K R R S U M L V T R S P K
M N A R T N M F X L Z U F Z S H Q Y Z R
Q T M N W D P B K P M B R Z K R V J H B
```

ANAGNOS	DEVIL	JAMES	OBEDIENCE	THREE
ANGEL	DICTIONARY	JIMMY	PAPA	TOOTH
ANNE	DOCTOR	KATE	PERCY	TRAIN
BELL	DOLLS	KELLER	PERKINS	TUSCUMBIA
BITE	EYELIDS	KEY	PITCHER	TWENTY
BOSTON	FOREVER	LADDER	PITY	TWENTYFIVE
BUTTONS	GARDEN	LANGUAGE	RATS	VINEY
CARRIAGE	GIBSON	MARTHA	RING	WATER
CHEEK	GIVING	MILDRED	SCISSORS	
CRAMP	GLASSES	MOUSETRAP	SULLIVAN	
CROCHET	HELEN	NAPKIN	TEACHER	
DEADHOUSE	IVY	NEEDLE	TEWKSBURY	

Miracle Worker Word Search 3 Answer Key

ANAGNOS	DEVIL	JAMES	OBEDIENCE	THREE
ANGEL	DICTIONARY	JIMMY	PAPA	TOOTH
ANNE	DOCTOR	KATE	PERCY	TRAIN
BELL	DOLLS	KELLER	PERKINS	TUSCUMBIA
BITE	EYELIDS	KEY	PITCHER	TWENTY
BOSTON	FOREVER	LADDER	PITY	TWENTYFIVE
BUTTONS	GARDEN	LANGUAGE	RATS	VINEY
CARRIAGE	GIBSON	MARTHA	RING	WATER
CHEEK	GIVING	MILDRED	SCISSORS	
CRAMP	GLASSES	MOUSETRAP	SULLIVAN	
CROCHET	HELEN	NAPKIN	TEACHER	
DEADHOUSE	IVY	NEEDLE	TEWKSBURY	

Miracle Worker Word Search 4

```
S C I S S O R S P N A P K I N J A M E S
J J K E S G D J V I H P M G D G P X G J N
B F E T M Q Y B P T O C O H L I H N B W
T V L M C W Y L Y R C B U E E G B R V R
H B L A D K U M R A N H E S E Q S Q H
V N E L W C W U A N M B W E D E K F O C
N R R G S L B V C Y J K U T R I T V X N
Z H M U V S I C R X G G X T D P E R S N
V W T D K L D A O R X Y P S T F W N A M
V J C W L N R C Q Z N P C V O H L C P
M K E U R O H R H E N L T H M T N J V E
H T S V I W E I E L V Q D C Y E B S W R
G H S T G A E A T D W X M B E A G Y Y X
A J C R G T R G M E V E O Y N C T C G T
R I Q T C E H E A E N S C V I H R N D R
D O C T O R T W E N T Y F I V E I K E Y
E T S Z A O A P A O A O V B P R B G A T
N H H T S B T M N M R G A N Q G B A R D J
D P S N E L E H P E I V N X U S E H S
E S I D L T V L E B L I O G C Y D O B
V N B T A Z Y E L R V D N S E F D U T
I T I K Y C R Q H A I K A R L J L A S T
L V T P X P K J P G W L I I E C Q L E G
F B E N P K B A Y G S C D N V D K B Q H
T R A I N C P D O L L S P J S J I M M Y
```

ANAGNOS
ANGEL
ANNE
BELL
BITE
BOSTON
BUTTONS
CARRIAGE
CHEEK
CRAMP
CROCHET
DEADHOUSE

DEVIL
DICTIONARY
DOCTOR
DOLLS
EYELIDS
FOREVER
GARDEN
GIBSON
GIVING
GLASSES
HELEN
IVY

JAMES
JIMMY
KATE
KELLER
KEY
LADDER
LANGUAGE
MARTHA
MILDRED
MOUSETRAP
NAPKIN
NEEDLE

OBEDIENCE
PAPA
PERCY
PERKINS
PITCHER
PITY
RATS
RING
SCISSORS
SULLIVAN
TEACHER
TEWKSBURY

THREE
TOOTH
TRAIN
TUSCUMBIA
TWENTY
TWENTYFIVE
VINEY
WATER

Miracle Worker Word Search 4 Answer Key

ANAGNOS	DEVIL	JAMES	OBEDIENCE	THREE
ANGEL	DICTIONARY	JIMMY	PAPA	TOOTH
ANNE	DOCTOR	KATE	PERCY	TRAIN
BELL	DOLLS	KELLER	PERKINS	TUSCUMBIA
BITE	EYELIDS	KEY	PITCHER	TWENTY
BOSTON	FOREVER	LADDER	PITY	TWENTYFIVE
BUTTONS	GARDEN	LANGUAGE	RATS	VINEY
CARRIAGE	GIBSON	MARTHA	RING	WATER
CHEEK	GIVING	MILDRED	SCISSORS	
CRAMP	GLASSES	MOUSETRAP	SULLIVAN	
CROCHET	HELEN	NAPKIN	TEACHER	
DEADHOUSE	IVY	NEEDLE	TEWKSBURY	

Miracle Worker Crossword 1

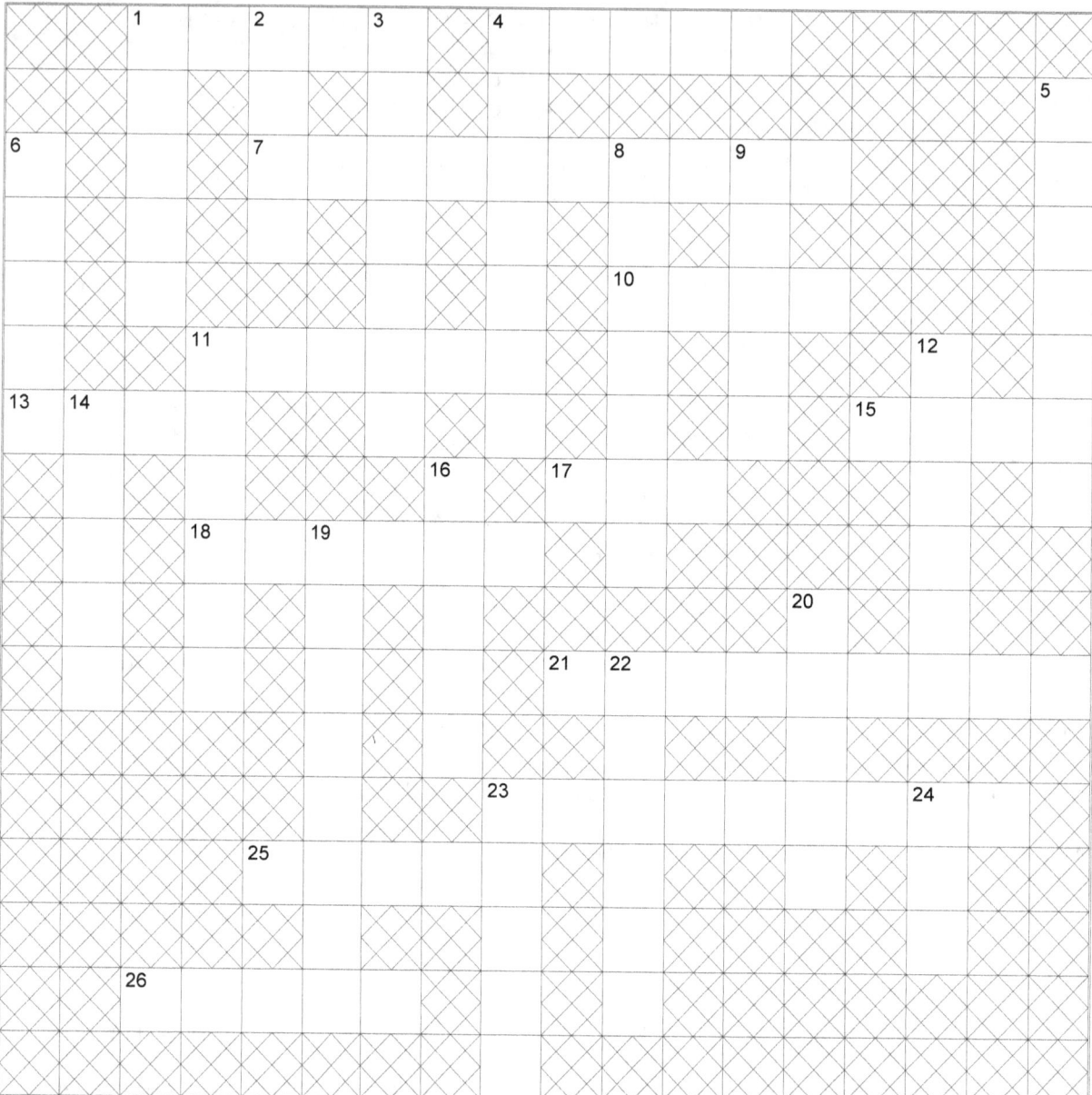

Across
1. Number of acts in this play
4. Helen puts her fingers in his mouth
7. Number of dollars a week Annie is paid
10. Going away present from Anagnos
11. Used to jab Annie
13. Sign for Captain Keller
15. Helen does this to her fingers in her mouth
17. Dropped by Helen into the well
18. Views women as the flowers of civilization: Captain ___
21. Gateway through which knowledge enters the mind
23. Town in AL where Kellers reside
25. Breakthrough word for Helen
26. A touch here means Kate

Down
1. It was knocked out when Helen hit Annie with the doll
2. Playthings for Annie and Jimmy in asylum
3. Doll blind girls give Annie for Helen has movable ___
4. Needed to be refilled at the pump
5. Helen made a string of wool doing this craft
6. Annie has this from signing to Helen: writer's ___
8. Promise of love to Jimmy and then Helen
9. Negro servant
11. Folded by Helen
12. Playwright
14. Baby Martha
16. Like a little safe, locked, that no one can open
19. Is to the mind more than light is to the eye
20. Haunting voice in Annie's mind
22. Perkins Institute location
23. How Annie traveled from Boston to Alabama
24. Keller estate in Alabama: ___ Green

Miracle Worker Crossword 1 Answer Key

	1 T	H	2 R	E	3 E		4 P	E	R	C	Y		
		O		A		Y		I					5 C
6 C	O	7 T	W	E	N	T	Y	F	I	8 V	E		R
R		T		S		L		C		O	I		O
A		H			I		H	10 R	I	N	G		C
M			11 N	E	E	D	L	E		E		12 G	H
13 P	14 A	P	A			S		R		V		15 B	I	T	E
	N		P			16 H		17 K	E	Y		B			T
	G		18 K	E	19 L	L	E	R				S			
	E		I		A					20 J		O			
	L		N		N	E		21 O	22 B	E	D	I	E	N	C	E
			G		N			O		M				
			U			23 T	U	S	C	U	M	B	24 I	A
		25 W	A	T	E	R		T		Y			V
			G			A		O					Y
		26 C	H	E	E	K		N				
						N						

Across
1. Number of acts in this play
4. Helen puts her fingers in his mouth
7. Number of dollars a week Annie is paid
10. Going away present from Anagnos
11. Used to jab Annie
13. Sign for Captain Keller
15. Helen does this to her fingers in her mouth
17. Dropped by Helen into the well
18. Views women as the flowers of civilization: Captain ___
21. Gateway through which knowledge enters the mind
23. Town in AL where Kellers reside
25. Breakthrough word for Helen
26. A touch here means Kate

Down
1. It was knocked out when Helen hit Annie with the doll
2. Playthings for Annie and Jimmy in asylum
3. Doll blind girls give Annie for Helen has movable ___
4. Needed to be refilled at the pump
5. Helen made a string of wool doing this craft
6. Annie has this from signing to Helen: writer's ___
8. Promise of love to Jimmy and then Helen
9. Negro servant
11. Folded by Helen
12. Playwright
14. Baby Martha
16. Like a little safe, locked, that no one can open
19. Is to the mind more than light is to the eye
20. Haunting voice in Annie's mind
22. Perkins Institute location
23. How Annie traveled from Boston to Alabama
24. Keller estate in Alabama: ___ Green

Miracle Worker Crossword 2

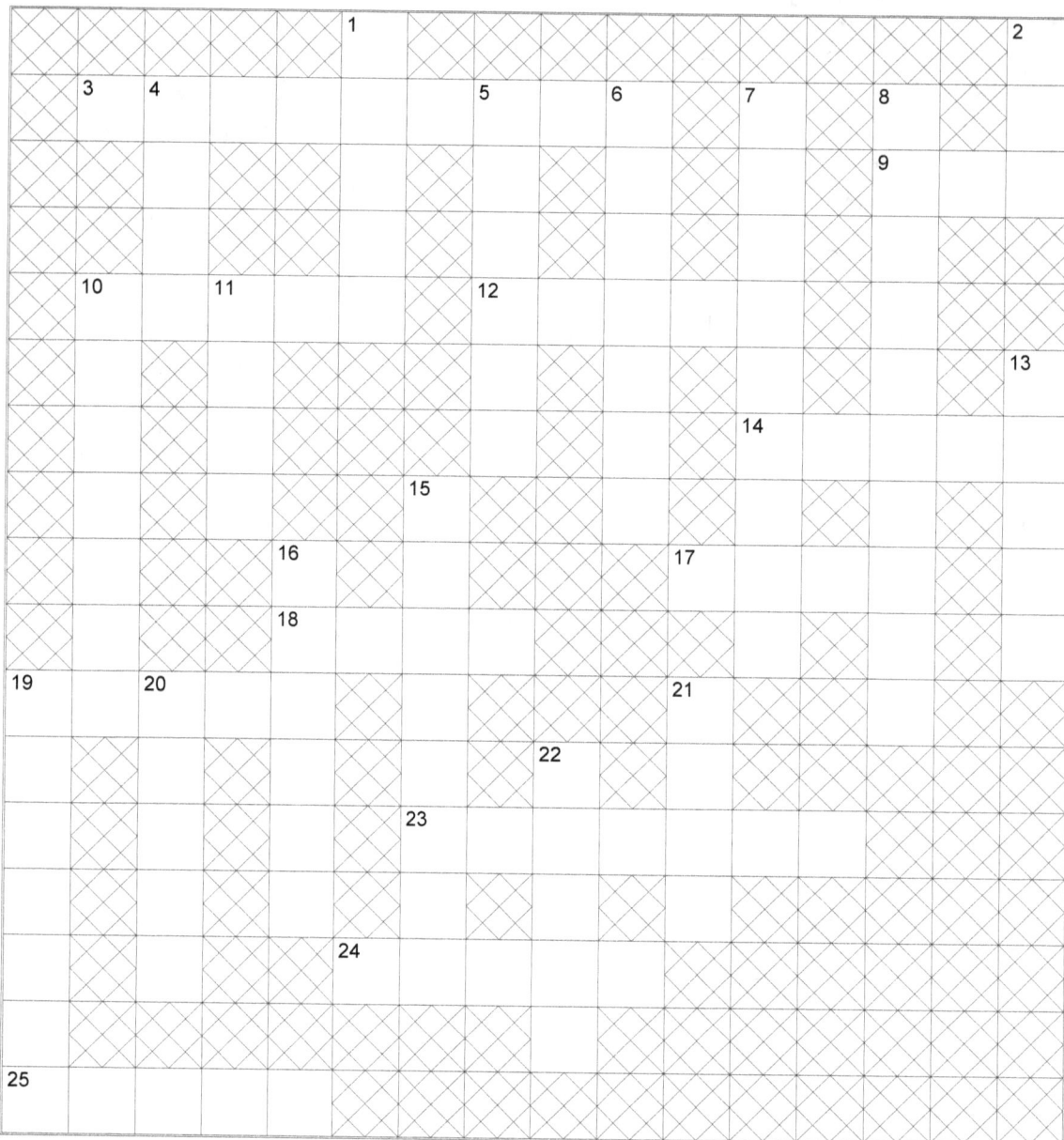

Across
3. Gateway through which knowledge enters the mind
9. Keller estate in Alabama: ___ Green
10. Helen puts her fingers in his mouth
12. Martha and Percy play with paper ___
14. It was knocked out when Helen hit Annie with the doll
17. Sign for Captain Keller
18. She has not loved a soul since her brother's death
19. Annie has this from signing to Helen: writer's ___
23. Annie's mentor from Perkins Institute
24. Like a little safe, locked, that no one can open
25. Number of acts in this play

Down
1. Negro servant
2. Dropped by Helen into the well
4. Helen does this to her fingers in her mouth
5. Used to jab Annie
6. Doll blind girls give Annie for Helen has movable ___
7. Helen's mind worked like one
8. Used by Annie to spell correctly
10. Needed to be refilled at the pump
11. Playthings for Annie and Jimmy in asylum
13. A touch here means Kate
15. Is to the mind more than light is to the eye
16. Folded by Helen
19. Helen made a string of wool doing this craft
20. Baby Martha
21. Going away present from Anagnos
22. Breakthrough word for Helen

Miracle Worker Crossword 2 Answer Key

					1 V						2 K
	3 O	4 B	E	D	I	5 E	N	6 C	E	7 M	8 D	E
		I			N		E		Y		O	9 I	V	Y
		T			E		E		E		U	C
	10 P	E	11 R	C	Y		12 D	O	L	L	S	T
		I		A				L		I		E		13 C
		T		T				E		D		14 T	O	O	T	H
		C		S		15 L				S		R		N		E
					16 N		A				17 P	A	P	A
		H		18 A	N	N	E				P		R		K
19 C		20 R	A	M	P		G				21 R			Y
R		A		N		K		U		22 W		I
O		23 A	N	A	G	N	O	S
C		G		I		G		T		G
H		E		N		24 H	E	L	E	N
E		L								R
25 T	H	R	E	E

Across
3. Gateway through which knowledge enters the mind
9. Keller estate in Alabama: ___ Green
10. Helen puts her fingers in his mouth
12. Martha and Percy play with paper ___
14. It was knocked out when Helen hit Annie with the doll
17. Sign for Captain Keller
18. She has not loved a soul since her brother's death
19. Annie has this from signing to Helen: writer's ___
23. Annie's mentor from Perkins Institute
24. Like a little safe, locked, that no one can open
25. Number of acts in this play

Down
1. Negro servant
2. Dropped by Helen into the well
4. Helen does this to her fingers in her mouth
5. Used to jab Annie
6. Doll blind girls give Annie for Helen has movable ___
7. Helen's mind worked like one
8. Used by Annie to spell correctly
10. Needed to be refilled at the pump
11. Playthings for Annie and Jimmy in asylum
13. A touch here means Kate
15. Is to the mind more than light is to the eye
16. Folded by Helen
19. Helen made a string of wool doing this craft
20. Baby Martha
21. Going away present from Anagnos
22. Breakthrough word for Helen

Miracle Worker Crossword 3

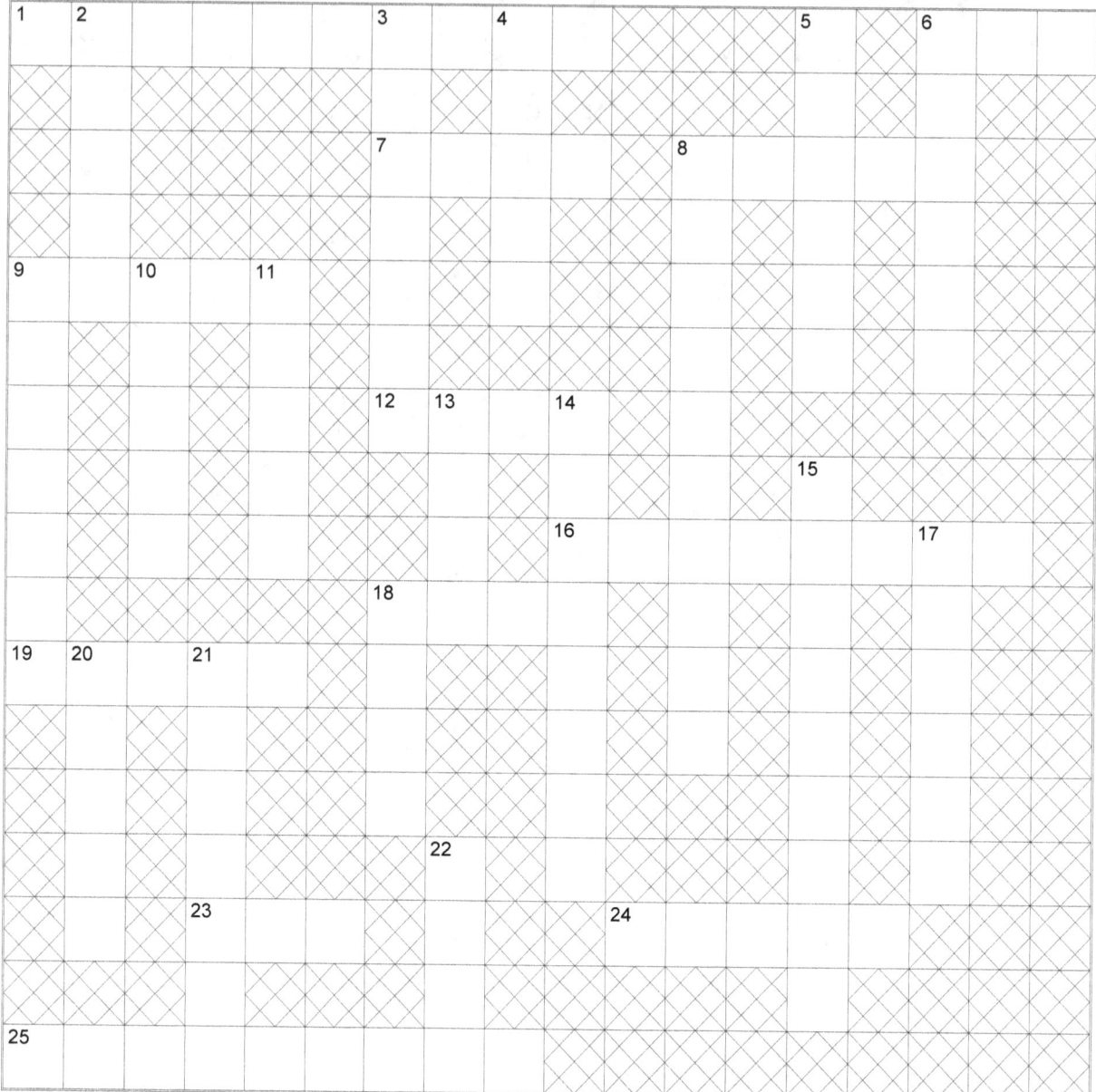

Across
1. Number of dollars a week Annie is paid
6. Dropped by Helen into the well
7. Going away present from Anagnos
8. Annie called Helen this after she hid the room key
9. Annie has this from signing to Helen: writer's ___
12. Playthings for Annie and Jimmy in asylum
16. Is to the mind more than light is to the eye
18. Used by Percy to alert family of Helen's outburst
19. Number of acts in this play
23. Keller estate in Alabama: ___ Green
24. How Annie traveled from Boston to Alabama
25. Helen's mind worked like one

Down
2. Breakthrough word for Helen
3. Promise of love to Jimmy and then Helen
4. Negro servant
5. Original sin according to Annie: ___ up
6. Views women as the flowers of civilization: Captain ___
8. Used by Annie to spell correctly
9. Helen made a string of wool doing this craft
10. Baby Martha
11. Helen puts her fingers in his mouth
13. She has not loved a soul since her brother's death
14. Anne's last name
15. Town in AL where Kellers reside
17. Playwright
18. Helen does this to her fingers in her mouth
20. Like a little safe, locked, that no one can open
21. Doll blind girls give Annie for Helen has movable ___
22. Sign for Captain Keller

Miracle Worker Crossword 3 Answer Key

	1 T	2 W	E	N	T	3 Y	F	4 I	V	E			5 G		6 K	E	Y
		A				O		I					I		E		
		T				7 R	I	N	G			8 D	E	V	I	L	
		E				E		E				I			L		
9 C	R	10 A	M	11 P		V		Y				C		N	E		
R		N		E		E						T		G	R		
O		G		R		12 R	13 A	T	14 S			I					
C		E		C			N		U				15 T			17	
H		L		Y			N		16 L	A	N	G	U	A	G	E	
E						18 B	E	L	L			A		S		I	
19 T	20 H	21 R	E	E		I			I			R		C		B	
	E	Y				T			V			Y		U		S	
	L	E				E			A					M		O	
	E	L				22 P			N					B		N	
	N	23 I	V	Y		A			24 T	R	A	I	N				
		D				P						A					
25 M	O	U	S	E	T	R	A	P									

Across
1. Number of dollars a week Annie is paid
6. Dropped by Helen into the well
7. Going away present from Anagnos
8. Annie called Helen this after she hid the room key
9. Annie has this from signing to Helen: writer's ___
12. Playthings for Annie and Jimmy in asylum
16. Is to the mind more than light is to the eye
18. Used by Percy to alert family of Helen's outburst
19. Number of acts in this play
23. Keller estate in Alabama: ___ Green
24. How Annie traveled from Boston to Alabama
25. Helen's mind worked like one

Down
2. Breakthrough word for Helen
3. Promise of love to Jimmy and then Helen
4. Negro servant
5. Original sin according to Annie: ___ up
6. Views women as the flowers of civilization: Captain ___
8. Used by Annie to spell correctly
9. Helen made a string of wool doing this craft
10. Baby Martha
11. Helen puts her fingers in his mouth
13. She has not loved a soul since her brother's death
14. Anne's last name
15. Town in AL where Kellers reside
17. Playwright
18. Helen does this to her fingers in her mouth
20. Like a little safe, locked, that no one can open
21. Doll blind girls give Annie for Helen has movable ___
22. Sign for Captain Keller

Miracle Worker Crossword 4

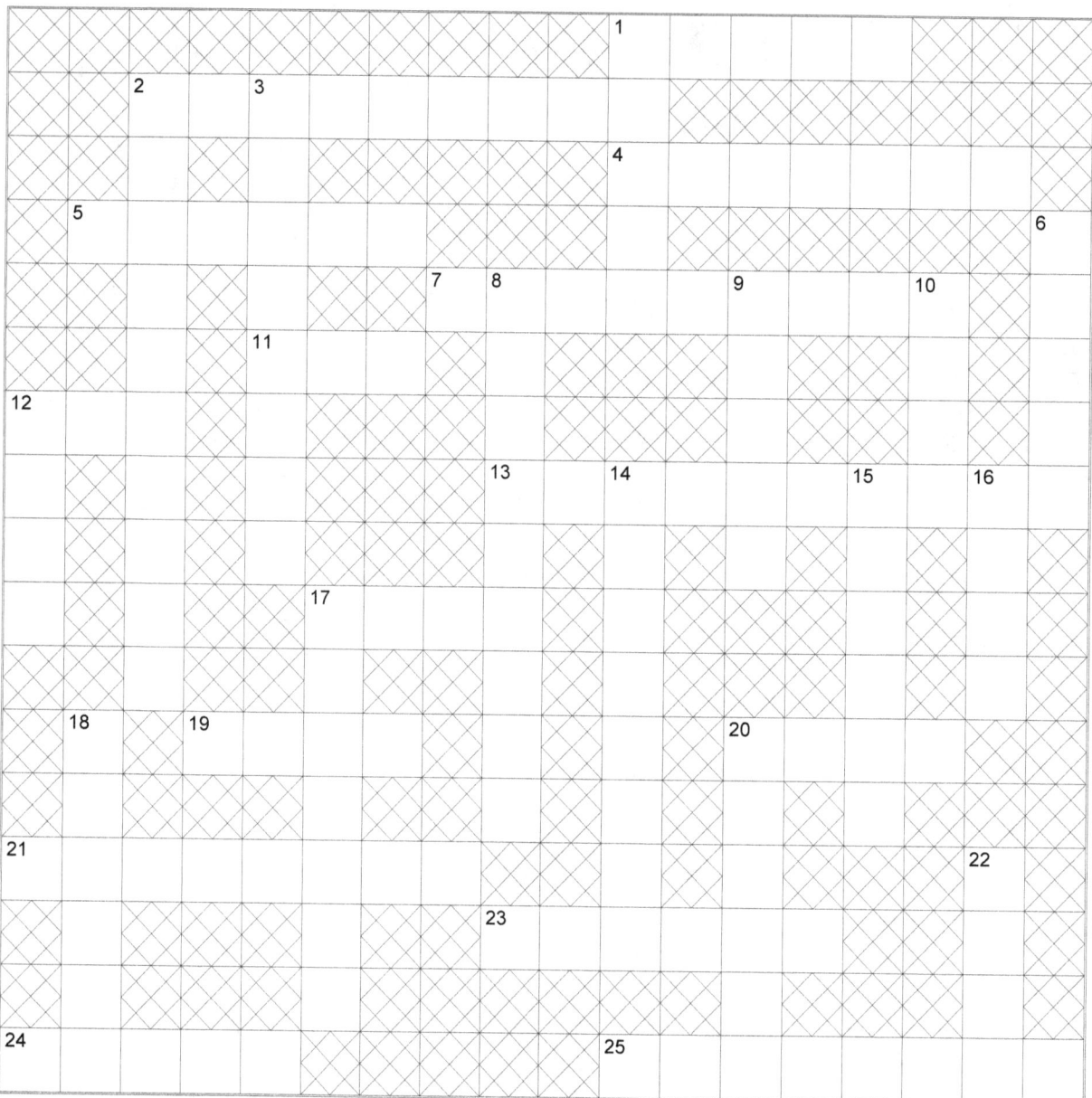

Across
1. Haunting voice in Annie's mind
2. Town in AL where Kellers reside
4. Helen's younger sibling
5. Views women as the flowers of civilization: Captain ___
7. Helen's mind worked like one
11. Keller estate in Alabama: ___ Green
12. Dropped by Helen into the well
13. Used by Annie to spell correctly
17. Helen does this to her fingers in her mouth
19. Captain wishes Annie would show some
20. Used by Percy to alert family of Helen's outburst
21. Taken from Martha forcefully by Helen
23. Governess's age
24. Annie has this from signing to Helen: writer's ___
25. Is to the mind more than light is to the eye

Down
1. Thinks half-sister Helen should be in asylum
2. Number of dollars a week Annie is paid
3. Anne's last name
6. Helen puts her fingers in his mouth
8. Gateway through which knowledge enters the mind
9. How Annie traveled from Boston to Alabama
10. Sign for Captain Keller
12. A woman steeled in grief
14. Driven to pick up Annie at the train station
15. Used to jab Annie
16. Playthings for Annie and Jimmy in asylum
17. Torn off Aunt Ev's dress by Helen for doll's eyes
18. Diagnoses baby Helen with acute congestion
20. Perkins Institute location
22. Going away present from Anagnos

Miracle Worker Crossword 4 Answer Key

							¹J	I	M	M	Y		
	²T	U	³S	C	U	M	B	I	A				
	W		U				⁴M	I	L	D	R	E	D
⁵K	E	L	L	E	R		E						⁶P
	N		L			⁷M	⁸O	U	S	E	⁹T	R	A	¹⁰P	E
	T		¹¹I	V	Y		B				R			A	R
¹²K	E	Y		V			E				A			P	C
A		F		A			¹³D	I	¹⁴C	T	I	¹⁵O	N	¹⁶A	R	Y
T		I		N			I		A		N		E		A	
E		V		¹⁷B	I	T	E		R			E		T
		E		U			N		R			D		S
	¹⁸D		¹⁹P	I	T	Y		C		²⁰B	E	L	L
	O			T				E		O		E	
²¹S	C	I	S	S	O	R	S		G		S			²²R
	T			N			²³T	W	E	N	T	Y		I
	O			S							O		N
²⁴C	R	A	M	P					²⁵L	A	N	G	U	A	G	E

Across
1. Haunting voice in Annie's mind
2. Town in AL where Kellers reside
4. Helen's younger sibling
5. Views women as the flowers of civilization: Captain ___
7. Helen's mind worked like one
11. Keller estate in Alabama: ___ Green
12. Dropped by Helen into the well
13. Used by Annie to spell correctly
17. Helen does this to her fingers in her mouth
19. Captain wishes Annie would show some
20. Used by Percy to alert family of Helen's outburst
21. Taken from Martha forcefully by Helen
23. Governess's age
24. Annie has this from signing to Helen: writer's ___
25. Is to the mind more than light is to the eye

Down
1. Thinks half-sister Helen should be in asylum
2. Number of dollars a week Annie is paid
3. Anne's last name
6. Helen puts her fingers in his mouth
8. Gateway through which knowledge enters the mind
9. How Annie traveled from Boston to Alabama
10. Sign for Captain Keller
12. A woman steeled in grief
14. Driven to pick up Annie at the train station
15. Used to jab Annie
16. Playthings for Annie and Jimmy in asylum
17. Torn off Aunt Ev's dress by Helen for doll's eyes
18. Diagnoses baby Helen with acute congestion
20. Perkins Institute location
22. Going away present from Anagnos

Miracle Worker

JAMES	SULLIVAN	FOREVER	PITCHER	KATE
CARRIAGE	TWENTY-FIVE	KEY	TOOTH	BITE
GARDEN	RING	FREE SPACE	DICTIONARY	TWENTY
KELLER	BUTTONS	ANAGNOS	SCISSORS	CRAMP
PAPA	LANGUAGE	MARTHA	DEADHOUSE	ANGEL

Miracle Worker

GLASSES	TRAIN	DOCTOR	DOLLS	EYELIDS
OBEDIENCE	CROCHET	WATER	MOUSETRAP	JIMMY
NEEDLE	MILDRED	FREE SPACE	BELL	VINEY
TEACHER	GIBSON	TUSCUMBIA	HELEN	LADDER
RATS	THREE	PITY	CHEEK	IVY

Miracle Worker

VINEY	DICTIONARY	JAMES	IVY	TOOTH
EYELIDS	FOREVER	WATER	DOLLS	TWENTY-FIVE
DEVIL	ANGEL	FREE SPACE	OBEDIENCE	BELL
ANNE	KELLER	ANAGNOS	NAPKIN	GIBSON
LADDER	BOSTON	TWENTY	SCISSORS	TUSCUMBIA

Miracle Worker

PITY	PAPA	TRAIN	SULLIVAN	CARRIAGE
THREE	GIVING	DOCTOR	PITCHER	BITE
RATS	KATE	FREE SPACE	DEADHOUSE	PERCY
CRAMP	CROCHET	CHEEK	MILDRED	KEY
TEACHER	PERKINS	NEEDLE	MOUSETRAP	LANGUAGE

Miracle Worker

MOUSETRAP	TRAIN	LADDER	NEEDLE	BOSTON
TWENTY	EYELIDS	PITY	THREE	CARRIAGE
PITCHER	BELL	FREE SPACE	CHEEK	PERCY
GARDEN	RATS	JIMMY	KEY	GIVING
BITE	CROCHET	DICTIONARY	SULLIVAN	MILDRED

Miracle Worker

TEACHER	CRAMP	TUSCUMBIA	ANNE	GLASSES
RING	ANGEL	KATE	TWENTY-FIVE	DEADHOUSE
BUTTONS	GIBSON	FREE SPACE	WATER	TOOTH
SCISSORS	FOREVER	MARTHA	KELLER	DOCTOR
TEWKSBURY	JAMES	LANGUAGE	HELEN	PERKINS

Miracle Worker

TWENTYFIVE	ANAGNOS	JAMES	BITE	SULLIVAN
GLASSES	CHEEK	ANGEL	KATE	TOOTH
CRAMP	FOREVER	FREE SPACE	GIBSON	DOCTOR
BOSTON	RATS	MARTHA	TUSCUMBIA	LADDER
GARDEN	EYELIDS	CROCHET	DICTIONARY	GIVING

Miracle Worker

LANGUAGE	PERKINS	WATER	PERCY	JIMMY
IVY	NEEDLE	MILDRED	TWENTY	PITY
PITCHER	ANNE	FREE SPACE	KELLER	TEWKSBURY
CARRIAGE	TRAIN	NAPKIN	TEACHER	DEVIL
THREE	DOLLS	SCISSORS	KEY	BUTTONS

Miracle Worker

PITY	GARDEN	MARTHA	GIBSON	BELL
LANGUAGE	TOOTH	DOLLS	PAPA	NEEDLE
KATE	FOREVER	FREE SPACE	RING	MILDRED
KEY	BOSTON	HELEN	RATS	ANAGNOS
NAPKIN	IVY	DICTIONARY	EYELIDS	DOCTOR

Miracle Worker

DEVIL	CRAMP	CROCHET	ANGEL	DEADHOUSE
PERKINS	CHEEK	TUSCUMBIA	ANNE	TRAIN
LADDER	CARRIAGE	FREE SPACE	PERCY	KELLER
SULLIVAN	TWENTYFIVE	BITE	GLASSES	TEWKSBURY
BUTTONS	JIMMY	JAMES	MOUSETRAP	OBEDIENCE

Miracle Worker

WATER	PITCHER	OBEDIENCE	VINEY	GARDEN
DOCTOR	BELL	MARTHA	DEVIL	BOSTON
IVY	PERCY	FREE SPACE	KATE	DEADHOUSE
CROCHET	TUSCUMBIA	MILDRED	HELEN	CARRIAGE
JAMES	MOUSETRAP	CRAMP	ANNE	RATS

Miracle Worker

RING	JIMMY	NEEDLE	GIVING	KELLER
PITY	KEY	TEWKSBURY	SULLIVAN	TOOTH
FOREVER	PERKINS	FREE SPACE	TEACHER	GIBSON
ANAGNOS	GLASSES	LADDER	ANGEL	LANGUAGE
TRAIN	THREE	TWENTY	CHEEK	DICTIONARY

Miracle Worker

DEADHOUSE	CHEEK	LADDER	PERCY	MOUSETRAP
VINEY	DOLLS	WATER	CRAMP	KATE
PAPA	TEWKSBURY	FREE SPACE	TWENTY	BOSTON
TUSCUMBIA	KELLER	DEVIL	OBEDIENCE	NAPKIN
FOREVER	RING	ANGEL	IVY	MILDRED

Miracle Worker

DICTIONARY	ANNE	CROCHET	JAMES	MARTHA
GIVING	SCISSORS	BUTTONS	THREE	TEACHER
TOOTH	TRAIN	FREE SPACE	GLASSES	NEEDLE
BITE	JIMMY	RATS	PERKINS	ANAGNOS
DOCTOR	SULLIVAN	CARRIAGE	HELEN	LANGUAGE

Miracle Worker

LADDER	CRAMP	CROCHET	FOREVER	MOUSETRAP
GLASSES	TWENTY-FIVE	PITCHER	PERCY	GARDEN
JIMMY	PITY	FREE SPACE	TOOTH	DOLLS
SULLIVAN	GIVING	BOSTON	KELLER	IVY
TWENTY	DEVIL	CARRIAGE	KEY	ANNE

Miracle Worker

BELL	CHEEK	EYELIDS	MILDRED	TUSCUMBIA
JAMES	RING	TEWKSBURY	ANAGNOS	GIBSON
LANGUAGE	TRAIN	FREE SPACE	KATE	VINEY
WATER	NAPKIN	SCISSORS	BUTTONS	DOCTOR
MARTHA	NEEDLE	BITE	PAPA	PERKINS

Miracle Worker

GLASSES	BELL	OBEDIENCE	NEEDLE	BOSTON
LANGUAGE	BITE	LADDER	HELEN	TRAIN
MARTHA	EYELIDS	FREE SPACE	TOOTH	KELLER
JIMMY	TEACHER	PAPA	KATE	PITCHER
BUTTONS	CARRIAGE	GIVING	WATER	IVY

Miracle Worker

DEADHOUSE	RATS	TWENTY	RING	CRAMP
SCISSORS	CHEEK	MILDRED	GIBSON	PERKINS
PERCY	THREE	FREE SPACE	TEWKSBURY	NAPKIN
ANNE	ANAGNOS	VINEY	TWENTY-FIVE	DOLLS
PITY	GARDEN	DEVIL	DICTIONARY	FOREVER

Miracle Worker

FOREVER	PAPA	BUTTONS	THREE	ANGEL
MOUSETRAP	GIVING	RING	VINEY	GLASSES
HELEN	RATS	FREE SPACE	BITE	ANNE
TEACHER	ANAGNOS	KELLER	DEADHOUSE	EYELIDS
IVY	OBEDIENCE	BOSTON	BELL	MARTHA

Miracle Worker

TEWKSBURY	TOOTH	PERCY	LADDER	TUSCUMBIA
GARDEN	SCISSORS	DICTIONARY	PITY	PITCHER
NEEDLE	JIMMY	FREE SPACE	DEVIL	WATER
NAPKIN	DOLLS	TRAIN	CARRIAGE	TWENTY
MILDRED	CHEEK	KATE	CRAMP	GIBSON

Miracle Worker

VINEY	CROCHET	BELL	PAPA	SCISSORS
DOLLS	GIBSON	OBEDIENCE	RATS	TOOTH
MILDRED	TWENTY	FREE SPACE	LANGUAGE	TRAIN
MOUSETRAP	BITE	DICTIONARY	JAMES	LADDER
CHEEK	NEEDLE	FOREVER	HELEN	EYELIDS

Miracle Worker

GLASSES	ANAGNOS	RING	TEACHER	PERCY
DOCTOR	ANNE	MARTHA	WATER	CRAMP
IVY	SULLIVAN	FREE SPACE	BOSTON	NAPKIN
GARDEN	GIVING	TUSCUMBIA	DEVIL	KELLER
THREE	TEWKSBURY	PERKINS	JIMMY	ANGEL

Miracle Worker

GIVING	TWENTY-FIVE	PITY	VINEY	BITE
KELLER	CROCHET	BUTTONS	GLASSES	ANAGNOS
SULLIVAN	OBEDIENCE	FREE SPACE	TOOTH	EYELIDS
TEWKSBURY	CARRIAGE	DICTIONARY	BELL	ANGEL
NEEDLE	DEADHOUSE	SCISSORS	NAPKIN	PAPA

Miracle Worker

RING	TRAIN	TWENTY	CHEEK	JAMES
ANNE	FOREVER	DOCTOR	WATER	GARDEN
DEVIL	PITCHER	FREE SPACE	HELEN	PERKINS
KATE	JIMMY	MOUSETRAP	TEACHER	CRAMP
GIBSON	RATS	IVY	PERCY	TUSCUMBIA

Miracle Worker

JIMMY	OBEDIENCE	RATS	FOREVER	TEACHER
ANNE	BOSTON	THREE	GARDEN	ANAGNOS
BELL	MARTHA	FREE SPACE	DEADHOUSE	LADDER
NAPKIN	PAPA	PITY	WATER	DOCTOR
RING	MILDRED	NEEDLE	KATE	BITE

Miracle Worker

DICTIONARY	TUSCUMBIA	VINEY	KEY	JAMES
DOLLS	EYELIDS	TWENTY	HELEN	TWENTY-FIVE
SCISSORS	PERKINS	FREE SPACE	DEVIL	CARRIAGE
SULLIVAN	BUTTONS	KELLER	GIVING	CHEEK
CROCHET	TOOTH	IVY	LANGUAGE	ANGEL

Miracle Worker

TRAIN	CARRIAGE	PITCHER	MILDRED	BELL
JAMES	PAPA	KEY	JIMMY	RING
KATE	BITE	FREE SPACE	TOOTH	ANGEL
CRAMP	KELLER	PERKINS	MARTHA	ANAGNOS
TEWKSBURY	MOUSETRAP	LANGUAGE	FOREVER	TWENTY

Miracle Worker

HELEN	GLASSES	GARDEN	VINEY	CHEEK
RATS	CROCHET	DEADHOUSE	IVY	PERCY
TEACHER	THREE	FREE SPACE	PITY	DOLLS
OBEDIENCE	SULLIVAN	SCISSORS	WATER	LADDER
DOCTOR	GIVING	ANNE	BUTTONS	NAPKIN

Miracle Worker

PERCY	GIBSON	PERKINS	VINEY	LADDER
OBEDIENCE	KELLER	BOSTON	SCISSORS	JAMES
PAPA	DICTIONARY	FREE SPACE	JIMMY	KATE
LANGUAGE	TOOTH	IVY	BELL	TWENTY
PITCHER	CRAMP	DOLLS	TWENTY-FIVE	KEY

Miracle Worker

NAPKIN	TRAIN	DEVIL	ANGEL	CARRIAGE
ANNE	PITY	BUTTONS	ANAGNOS	BITE
NEEDLE	SULLIVAN	FREE SPACE	GIVING	MOUSETRAP
FOREVER	CHEEK	EYELIDS	MARTHA	GLASSES
TEACHER	TUSCUMBIA	RATS	MILDRED	GARDEN

Miracle Worker

OBEDIENCE	KATE	TEWKSBURY	CROCHET	DEVIL
PITCHER	TOOTH	GLASSES	JAMES	BOSTON
CHEEK	GIBSON	FREE SPACE	SCISSORS	LADDER
BELL	KELLER	HELEN	DOLLS	MARTHA
RATS	PERKINS	FOREVER	TWENTY	WATER

Miracle Worker

TUSCUMBIA	PERCY	VINEY	DOCTOR	PAPA
JIMMY	ANNE	GIVING	DEADHOUSE	KEY
IVY	NEEDLE	FREE SPACE	PITY	CRAMP
THREE	MOUSETRAP	TEACHER	ANGEL	LANGUAGE
RING	EYELIDS	MILDRED	TRAIN	TWENTY-FIVE

Miracle Worker Vocabulary Word List

No.	Word	Clue/Definition
1.	AFFLICTION	Hardship; problem
2.	ALMSHOUSE	Sanitarium
3.	AMIABLY	Agreeably; willingly
4.	APPRAISAL	Evaluation
5.	ASPERITY	Somewhat ill-tempered
6.	AVERSION	Distaste for; dislike for
7.	BAFFLED	Confused; bewildered
8.	BENIGN	Favorable; harmless
9.	BLANDLY	Flatly; tritely
10.	CARICATURE	Exaggerated model
11.	CHIVALROUS	Gentlemanly; gallant
12.	COMBATIVE	Inclined to fight
13.	COMPELLED	Obliged; made responsible
14.	COMPUNCTION	Shame; regret
15.	CONSPICUOUSLY	Clearly; obviously
16.	CONSUMMATELY	Absolutely; perfectly
17.	DEFERENTIAL	Respectful; obedient
18.	DEPRIVATION	Loss
19.	DESICCATED	Dried up
20.	DEVOUTNESS	Godliness; piety
21.	DIMINUTIVE	Small
22.	DISENGAGE	Release; undo
23.	DISHEVELED	Rumpled; untidy
24.	DOURLY	Drearily
25.	EMPHATIC	Pointed; insistent
26.	FACETIOUSLY	Flippant; smart-alecky
27.	FORLORN	Forsaken; abandoned
28.	FRIVOLOUS	Trivial; petty
29.	HAGGARD	Care worn; drawn
30.	IMPASSIVELY	Unemotionally
31.	IMPERCEPTIBLY	Unnoticeably; barely
32.	IMPERIOUS	Urgent; pressing
33.	IMPERTINENT	Rude; impolite
34.	IMPUDENCE	Boldness
35.	INARTICULATE	Wordless; silent
36.	INDIGNANTLY	Righteously angry
37.	INDOLENT	Idle; inactive
38.	INDULGENT	Permissive; lenient
39.	INEFFECTUAL	Useless
40.	INEXORABLY	Relentlessly; unyielding
41.	INTERMINABLE	Unending; ceaseless
42.	INTERPOSES	Intervenes; interferes
43.	INTIMATIONS	Allusions; hints
44.	INTRACTABLY	Inflexibly; in a headstrong manner
45.	IRRESOLUTE	Uncertain; hesitant
46.	JOVIAL	Jolly; happy
47.	LAMENTS	Moans; wails
48.	MANIPULATES	Maneuvers; moves
49.	MOROSELY	Gloomily; sullenly
50.	NETTLED	Bothered; peeved
51.	NONPLUSED	Bewildered; puzzled

Miracle Worker Vocabulary Word List Continued

No.	Word	Clue/Definition
52.	OBSTINATE	Stubborn; headstrong
53.	OCULIST	Eye doctor
54.	OMINOUSLY	Threateningly; darkly; gloomily
55.	PANTOMIME	Gestures without voice
56.	PAROXYSM	Fit; attack
57.	PLACATING	Satisfying; gratifying
58.	PLAINTIVELY	Sorrowfully; sadly
59.	PRIMER	Manual; handbook
60.	PROFFERED	Offered forth
61.	PUMMELS	Thrashes; beats
62.	RECOMMENCED	Repeated; began again
63.	RELINQUISHES	Resigns; gives up
64.	REPROACHFULLY	Disapprovingly; critically
65.	RESOLUTELY	Deliberately; willfully
66.	SOLICITUDE	Concern
67.	SPINSTER	Old, unmarried woman
68.	SWADDLED	Wrapped up
69.	TEMPERANCE	Moderation
70.	TRACHOMA	Inflammation of the eyelids
71.	TRANSFIXED	Motionless; frozen
72.	TREPIDATION	Fear; alarm
73.	TYRANT	Harsh, cruel leader
74.	UNAVAILING	Hopeless; futile
75.	UNKEMPT	Disorderly; messy
76.	UNOBSTRUCTED	In open view
77.	UNPERTURBED	Undisturbed; unbothered
78.	VALIANTLY	Bravely; courageously
79.	VEXEDLY	Irritatedly
80.	VIGIL	A watch
81.	VIVACIOUS	Lively; spirited
82.	VOLUMINOUS	Bulky; large
83.	WITHERING	Shrinking
84.	WOEBEGONE	Miserable; sorrowful
85.	WRITHES	Twists from pain; flails

Copyrighted

Miracle Worker Vocabulary Fill In The Blank 1

_____ 1. Wrapped up
_____ 2. Small
_____ 3. Old, unmarried woman
_____ 4. Threateningly; darkly; gloomily
_____ 5. Eye doctor
_____ 6. Undisturbed; unbothered
_____ 7. Moderation
_____ 8. Hardship; problem
_____ 9. Shrinking
_____ 10. Twists from pain; flails
_____ 11. Clearly; obviously
_____ 12. In open view
_____ 13. Moans; wails
_____ 14. Bewildered; puzzled
_____ 15. Agreeably; willingly
_____ 16. Uncertain; hesitant
_____ 17. Harsh, cruel leader
_____ 18. Drearily
_____ 19. Unending; ceaseless
_____ 20. Sorrowfully' sadly

Miracle Worker Vocabulary Fill In The Blank 1 Answer Key

SWADDLED	1. Wrapped up
DIMINUTIVE	2. Small
SPINSTER	3. Old, unmarried woman
OMINOUSLY	4. Threateningly; darkly; gloomily
OCULIST	5. Eye doctor
UNPERTURBED	6. Undisturbed; unbothered
TEMPERANCE	7. Moderation
AFFLICTION	8. Hardship; problem
WITHERING	9. Shrinking
WRITHES	10. Twists from pain; flails
CONSPICUOUSLY	11. Clearly; obviously
UNOBSTRUCTED	12. In open view
LAMENTS	13. Moans; wails
NONPLUSED	14. Bewildered; puzzled
AMIABLY	15. Agreeably; willingly
IRRESOLUTE	16. Uncertain; hesitant
TYRANT	17. Harsh, cruel leader
DOURLY	18. Drearily
INTERMINABLE	19. Unending; ceaseless
PLAINTIVELY	20. Sorrowfully' sadly

Miracle Worker Vocabulary Fill In The Blank 2

_____ 1. Permissive; lenient
_____ 2. Twists from pain; flails
_____ 3. Agreeably; willingly
_____ 4. Useless
_____ 5. Inclined to fight
_____ 6. Urgent; pressing
_____ 7. Pointed; insistent
_____ 8. Obliged; made responsible
_____ 9. Exaggerated model
_____ 10. Wordless; silent
_____ 11. Godliness; piety
_____ 12. Eye doctor
_____ 13. Inflexibly; in a headstrong manner
_____ 14. Righteously angry
_____ 15. Intervenes; interferes
_____ 16. Moderation
_____ 17. Gloomily; sullenly
_____ 18. Disapprovingly; critically
_____ 19. Wrapped up
_____ 20. Bothered; peeved

Miracle Worker Vocabulary Fill In The Blank 2 Answer Key

INDULGENT	1. Permissive; lenient
WRITHES	2. Twists from pain; flails
AMIABLY	3. Agreeably; willingly
INEFFECTUAL	4. Useless
COMBATIVE	5. Inclined to fight
IMPERIOUS	6. Urgent; pressing
EMPHATIC	7. Pointed; insistent
COMPELLED	8. Obliged; made responsible
CARICATURE	9. Exaggerated model
INARTICULATE	10. Wordless; silent
DEVOUTNESS	11. Godliness; piety
OCULIST	12. Eye doctor
INTRACTABLY	13. Inflexibly; in a headstrong manner
INDIGNANTLY	14. Righteously angry
INTERPOSES	15. Intervenes; interferes
TEMPERANCE	16. Moderation
MOROSELY	17. Gloomily; sullenly
REPROACHFULLY	18. Disapprovingly; critically
SWADDLED	19. Wrapped up
NETTLED	20. Bothered; peeved

Miracle Worker Vocabulary Fill In The Blank 3

_____ 1. Flippant; smart-alecky

_____ 2. Sorrowfully; sadly

_____ 3. Gloomily; sullenly

_____ 4. Threateningly; darkly; gloomily

_____ 5. Dried up

_____ 6. Pointed; insistent

_____ 7. Confused; bewildered

_____ 8. Favorable; harmless

_____ 9. Rude; impolite

_____ 10. Shame; regret

_____ 11. Gestures without voice

_____ 12. Gentlemanly; gallant

_____ 13. Twists from pain; flails

_____ 14. Unemotionally

_____ 15. Drearily

_____ 16. Stubborn; headstrong

_____ 17. A watch

_____ 18. Eye doctor

_____ 19. Exaggerated model

_____ 20. Unnoticeably; barely

Miracle Worker Vocabulary Fill In The Blank 3 Answer Key

FACETIOUSLY	1. Flippant; smart-alecky
PLAINTIVELY	2. Sorrowfully; sadly
MOROSELY	3. Gloomily; sullenly
OMINOUSLY	4. Threateningly; darkly; gloomily
DESICCATED	5. Dried up
EMPHATIC	6. Pointed; insistent
BAFFLED	7. Confused; bewildered
BENIGN	8. Favorable; harmless
IMPERTINENT	9. Rude; impolite
COMPUNCTION	10. Shame; regret
PANTOMIME	11. Gestures without voice
CHIVALROUS	12. Gentlemanly; gallant
WRITHES	13. Twists from pain; flails
IMPASSIVELY	14. Unemotionally
DOURLY	15. Drearily
OBSTINATE	16. Stubborn; headstrong
VIGIL	17. A watch
OCULIST	18. Eye doctor
CARICATURE	19. Exaggerated model
IMPERCEPTIBLY	20. Unnoticeably; barely

Miracle Worker Vocabulary Fill In The Blank 4

_____ 1. Trivial; petty
_____ 2. Hopeless; futile
_____ 3. Clearly; obviously
_____ 4. Unending; ceaseless
_____ 5. Pointed; insistent
_____ 6. Harsh, cruel leader
_____ 7. Wordless; silent
_____ 8. Offered forth
_____ 9. Repeated; began again
_____ 10. Evaluation
_____ 11. Inflammation of the eyelids
_____ 12. Shame; regret
_____ 13. Concern
_____ 14. Drearily
_____ 15. Disorderly; messy
_____ 16. Gestures without voice
_____ 17. Gentlemanly; gallant
_____ 18. Respectful; obedient
_____ 19. Bothered; peeved
_____ 20. Allusions; hints

Miracle Worker Vocabulary Fill In The Blank 4 Answer Key

FRIVOLOUS	1. Trivial; petty
UNAVAILING	2. Hopeless; futile
CONSPICUOUSLY	3. Clearly; obviously
INTERMINABLE	4. Unending; ceaseless
EMPHATIC	5. Pointed; insistent
TYRANT	6. Harsh, cruel leader
INARTICULATE	7. Wordless; silent
PROFFERED	8. Offered forth
RECOMMENCED	9. Repeated; began again
APPRAISAL	10. Evaluation
TRACHOMA	11. Inflammation of the eyelids
COMPUNCTION	12. Shame; regret
SOLICITUDE	13. Concern
DOURLY	14. Drearily
UNKEMPT	15. Disorderly; messy
PANTOMIME	16. Gestures without voice
CHIVALROUS	17. Gentlemanly; gallant
DEFERENTIAL	18. Respectful; obedient
NETTLED	19. Bothered; peeved
INTIMATIONS	20. Allusions; hints

Miracle Worker Vocabulary Matching 1

___ 1. DISENGAGE   A. Manual; handbook
___ 2. WITHERING   B. Release; undo
___ 3. IMPUDENCE   C. Resigns; gives up
___ 4. INEFFECTUAL   D. Miserable; sorrowful
___ 5. PLACATING   E. Shame; regret
___ 6. AVERSION   F. Distaste for; dislike for
___ 7. ASPERITY   G. Pointed; insistent
___ 8. COMPUNCTION   H. Somewhat ill-tempered
___ 9. RELINQUISHES   I. Bravely; courageously
___ 10. EMPHATIC   J. Moans; wails
___ 11. IMPERCEPTIBLY   K. Shrinking
___ 12. CARICATURE   L. Useless
___ 13. LAMENTS   M. Unnoticeably; barely
___ 14. DISHEVELED   N. Offered forth
___ 15. BENIGN   O. Agreeably; willingly
___ 16. SWADDLED   P. Relentlessly; unyielding
___ 17. INEXORABLY   Q. Favorable; harmless
___ 18. ALMSHOUSE   R. Rumpled; untidy
___ 19. AMIABLY   S. Boldness
___ 20. WOEBEGONE   T. Wrapped up
___ 21. UNOBSTRUCTED   U. Sanitarium
___ 22. PRIMER   V. Exaggerated model
___ 23. PAROXYSM   W. In open view
___ 24. PROFFERED   X. Fit; attack
___ 25. VALIANTLY   Y. Satisfying; gratifying

Miracle Worker Vocabulary Matching 1 Answer Key

B - 1.	DISENGAGE	A. Manual; handbook
K - 2.	WITHERING	B. Release; undo
S - 3.	IMPUDENCE	C. Resigns; gives up
L - 4.	INEFFECTUAL	D. Miserable; sorrowful
Y - 5.	PLACATING	E. Shame; regret
F - 6.	AVERSION	F. Distaste for; dislike for
H - 7.	ASPERITY	G. Pointed; insistent
E - 8.	COMPUNCTION	H. Somewhat ill-tempered
C - 9.	RELINQUISHES	I. Bravely; courageously
G - 10.	EMPHATIC	J. Moans; wails
M - 11.	IMPERCEPTIBLY	K. Shrinking
V - 12.	CARICATURE	L. Useless
J - 13.	LAMENTS	M. Unnoticeably; barely
R - 14.	DISHEVELED	N. Offered forth
Q - 15.	BENIGN	O. Agreeably; willingly
T - 16.	SWADDLED	P. Relentlessly; unyielding
P - 17.	INEXORABLY	Q. Favorable; harmless
U - 18.	ALMSHOUSE	R. Rumpled; untidy
O - 19.	AMIABLY	S. Boldness
D - 20.	WOEBEGONE	T. Wrapped up
W - 21.	UNOBSTRUCTED	U. Sanitarium
A - 22.	PRIMER	V. Exaggerated model
X - 23.	PAROXYSM	W. In open view
N - 24.	PROFFERED	X. Fit; attack
I - 25.	VALIANTLY	Y. Satisfying; gratifying

Miracle Worker Vocabulary Matching 2

___ 1. INDOLENT   A. Gentlemanly; gallant
___ 2. IMPERIOUS   B. Bravely; courageously
___ 3. CARICATURE   C. Inclined to fight
___ 4. AFFLICTION   D. Uncertain; hesitant
___ 5. FRIVOLOUS   E. Righteously angry
___ 6. TRACHOMA   F. Maneuvers; moves
___ 7. OBSTINATE   G. Irritatedly
___ 8. IRRESOLUTE   H. Trivial; petty
___ 9. PUMMELS   I. Clearly; obviously
___ 10. BAFFLED   J. Release; undo
___ 11. AMIABLY   K. Agreeably; willingly
___ 12. VEXEDLY   L. Rumpled; untidy
___ 13. PLACATING   M. Exaggerated model
___ 14. DISHEVELED   N. Thrashes; beats
___ 15. CONSPICUOUSLY   O. Confused; bewildered
___ 16. VOLUMINOUS   P. Stubborn; headstrong
___ 17. CHIVALROUS   Q. Wrapped up
___ 18. IMPERCEPTIBLY   R. Bulky; large
___ 19. MANIPULATES   S. Disapprovingly; critically
___ 20. REPROACHFULLY   T. Unnoticeably; barely
___ 21. DISENGAGE   U. Satisfying; gratifying
___ 22. COMBATIVE   V. Hardship; problem
___ 23. VALIANTLY   W. Idle; inactive
___ 24. SWADDLED   X. Inflammation of the eyelids
___ 25. INDIGNANTLY   Y. Urgent; pressing

Miracle Worker Vocabulary Matching 2 Answer Key

W - 1. INDOLENT	A.	Gentlemanly; gallant
Y - 2. IMPERIOUS	B.	Bravely; courageously
M - 3. CARICATURE	C.	Inclined to fight
V - 4. AFFLICTION	D.	Uncertain; hesitant
H - 5. FRIVOLOUS	E.	Righteously angry
X - 6. TRACHOMA	F.	Maneuvers; moves
P - 7. OBSTINATE	G.	Irritatedly
D - 8. IRRESOLUTE	H.	Trivial; petty
N - 9. PUMMELS	I.	Clearly; obviously
O - 10. BAFFLED	J.	Release; undo
K - 11. AMIABLY	K.	Agreeably; willingly
G - 12. VEXEDLY	L.	Rumpled; untidy
U - 13. PLACATING	M.	Exaggerated model
L - 14. DISHEVELED	N.	Thrashes; beats
I - 15. CONSPICUOUSLY	O.	Confused; bewildered
R - 16. VOLUMINOUS	P.	Stubborn; headstrong
A - 17. CHIVALROUS	Q.	Wrapped up
T - 18. IMPERCEPTIBLY	R.	Bulky; large
F - 19. MANIPULATES	S.	Disapprovingly; critically
S - 20. REPROACHFULLY	T.	Unnoticeably; barely
J - 21. DISENGAGE	U.	Satisfying; gratifying
C - 22. COMBATIVE	V.	Hardship; problem
B - 23. VALIANTLY	W.	Idle; inactive
Q - 24. SWADDLED	X.	Inflammation of the eyelids
E - 25. INDIGNANTLY	Y.	Urgent; pressing

Miracle Worker Vocabulary Matching 3

___ 1. PUMMELS   A. Inflammation of the eyelids
___ 2. DEPRIVATION   B. Maneuvers; moves
___ 3. TRANSFIXED   C. Flippant; smart-alecky
___ 4. INTIMATIONS   D. Bravely; courageously
___ 5. OCULIST   E. Offered forth
___ 6. AVERSION   F. Clearly; obviously
___ 7. TRACHOMA   G. Evaluation
___ 8. APPRAISAL   H. Allusions; hints
___ 9. PROFFERED   I. Eye doctor
___10. RESOLUTELY   J. Small
___11. SPINSTER   K. Moderation
___12. WOEBEGONE   L. Fit; attack
___13. NONPLUSED   M. Pointed; insistent
___14. PAROXYSM   N. Urgent; pressing
___15. EMPHATIC   O. Loss
___16. IMPERIOUS   P. Gestures without voice
___17. PLAINTIVELY   Q. Sorrowfully; sadly
___18. CONSPICUOUSLY   R. Old, unmarried woman
___19. MANIPULATES   S. Distaste for; dislike for
___20. TEMPERANCE   T. Motionless; frozen
___21. DIMINUTIVE   U. Thrashes; beats
___22. INTERMINABLE   V. Miserable; sorrowful
___23. PANTOMIME   W. Bewildered; puzzled
___24. VALIANTLY   X. Deliberately; willfully
___25. FACETIOUSLY   Y. Unending; ceaseless

Miracle Worker Vocabulary Matching 3 Answer Key

U - 1. PUMMELS	A.	Inflammation of the eyelids
O - 2. DEPRIVATION	B.	Maneuvers; moves
T - 3. TRANSFIXED	C.	Flippant; smart-alecky
H - 4. INTIMATIONS	D.	Bravely; courageously
I - 5. OCULIST	E.	Offered forth
S - 6. AVERSION	F.	Clearly; obviously
A - 7. TRACHOMA	G.	Evaluation
G - 8. APPRAISAL	H.	Allusions; hints
E - 9. PROFFERED	I.	Eye doctor
X - 10. RESOLUTELY	J.	Small
R - 11. SPINSTER	K.	Moderation
V - 12. WOEBEGONE	L.	Fit; attack
W - 13. NONPLUSED	M.	Pointed; insistent
L - 14. PAROXYSM	N.	Urgent; pressing
M - 15. EMPHATIC	O.	Loss
N - 16. IMPERIOUS	P.	Gestures without voice
Q - 17. PLAINTIVELY	Q.	Sorrowfully; sadly
F - 18. CONSPICUOUSLY	R.	Old, unmarried woman
B - 19. MANIPULATES	S.	Distaste for; dislike for
K - 20. TEMPERANCE	T.	Motionless; frozen
J - 21. DIMINUTIVE	U.	Thrashes; beats
Y - 22. INTERMINABLE	V.	Miserable; sorrowful
P - 23. PANTOMIME	W.	Bewildered; puzzled
D - 24. VALIANTLY	X.	Deliberately; willfully
C - 25. FACETIOUSLY	Y.	Unending; ceaseless

Miracle Worker Vocabulary Matching 4

___ 1. APPRAISAL   A. Harsh, cruel leader
___ 2. FORLORN   B. Gestures without voice
___ 3. UNOBSTRUCTED   C. Thrashes; beats
___ 4. DEVOUTNESS   D. Sanitarium
___ 5. TYRANT   E. Bewildered; puzzled
___ 6. COMPELLED   F. Useless
___ 7. MANIPULATES   G. Drearily
___ 8. FACETIOUSLY   H. Godliness; piety
___ 9. PUMMELS   I. Intervenes; interferes
___10. PANTOMIME   J. Forsaken; abandoned
___11. INTERPOSES   K. Agreeably; willingly
___12. NONPLUSED   L. Gloomily; sullenly
___13. OMINOUSLY   M. Obliged; made responsible
___14. INDOLENT   N. Flippant; smart-alecky
___15. WOEBEGONE   O. Threateningly; darkly; gloomily
___16. EMPHATIC   P. Manual; handbook
___17. AMIABLY   Q. Relentlessly; unyielding
___18. INEXORABLY   R. Evaluation
___19. DESICCATED   S. Pointed; insistent
___20. INEFFECTUAL   T. In open view
___21. DOURLY   U. Dried up
___22. VOLUMINOUS   V. Maneuvers; moves
___23. PRIMER   W. Bulky; large
___24. ALMSHOUSE   X. Idle; inactive
___25. MOROSELY   Y. Miserable; sorrowful

Miracle Worker Vocabulary Matching 4 Answer Key

R - 1. APPRAISAL		A. Harsh, cruel leader
J - 2. FORLORN		B. Gestures without voice
T - 3. UNOBSTRUCTED		C. Thrashes; beats
H - 4. DEVOUTNESS		D. Sanitarium
A - 5. TYRANT		E. Bewildered; puzzled
M - 6. COMPELLED		F. Useless
V - 7. MANIPULATES		G. Drearily
N - 8. FACETIOUSLY		H. Godliness; piety
C - 9. PUMMELS		I. Intervenes; interferes
B - 10. PANTOMIME		J. Forsaken; abandoned
I - 11. INTERPOSES		K. Agreeably; willingly
E - 12. NONPLUSED		L. Gloomily; sullenly
O - 13. OMINOUSLY		M. Obliged; made responsible
X - 14. INDOLENT		N. Flippant; smart-alecky
Y - 15. WOEBEGONE		O. Threateningly; darkly; gloomily
S - 16. EMPHATIC		P. Manual; handbook
K - 17. AMIABLY		Q. Relentlessly; unyielding
Q - 18. INEXORABLY		R. Evaluation
U - 19. DESICCATED		S. Pointed; insistent
F - 20. INEFFECTUAL		T. In open view
G - 21. DOURLY		U. Dried up
W - 22. VOLUMINOUS		V. Maneuvers; moves
P - 23. PRIMER		W. Bulky; large
D - 24. ALMSHOUSE		X. Idle; inactive
L - 25. MOROSELY		Y. Miserable; sorrowful

Miracle Worker Vocabulary Magic Squares 1

Match the definition with the vocabulary word. Put your answers in the magic squares below. When your answers are correct, all columns and rows will add to the same number.

A. SOLICITUDE
B. TRANSFIXED
C. RECOMMENCED
D. AMIABLY
E. MOROSELY
F. RESOLUTELY
G. RELINQUISHES
H. IMPASSIVELY
I. DESICCATED
J. DEVOUTNESS
K. SPINSTER
L. COMPELLED
M. WRITHES
N. VIGIL
O. APPRAISAL
P. AFFLICTION

1. Unemotionally
2. Twists from pain; flails
3. Motionless; frozen
4. Old, unmarried woman
5. Godliness; piety
6. Repeated; began again
7. Hardship; problem
8. Gloomily; sullenly
9. Evaluation
10. Deliberately; willfully
11. Dried up
12. Agreeably; willingly
13. Concern
14. Obliged; made responsible
15. Resigns; gives up
16. A watch

A=	B=	C=	D=
E=	F=	G=	H=
I=	J=	K=	L=
M=	N=	O=	P=

Miracle Worker Vocabulary Magic Squares 1 Answer Key

Match the definition with the vocabulary word. Put your answers in the magic squares below. When your answers are correct, all columns and rows will add to the same number.

A. SOLICITUDE
B. TRANSFIXED
C. RECOMMENCED
D. AMIABLY
E. MOROSELY
F. RESOLUTELY
G. RELINQUISHES
H. IMPASSIVELY
I. DESICCATED
J. DEVOUTNESS
K. SPINSTER
L. COMPELLED
M. WRITHES
N. VIGIL
O. APPRAISAL
P. AFFLICTION

1. Unemotionally
2. Twists from pain; flails
3. Motionless; frozen
4. Old, unmarried woman
5. Godliness; piety
6. Repeated; began again
7. Hardship; problem
8. Gloomily; sullenly
9. Evaluation
10. Deliberately; willfully
11. Dried up
12. Agreeably; willingly
13. Concern
14. Obliged; made responsible
15. Resigns; gives up
16. A watch

A=13	B=3	C=6	D=12
E=8	F=10	G=15	H=1
I=11	J=5	K=4	L=14
M=2	N=16	O=9	P=7

Miracle Worker Vocabulary Magic Squares 2

Match the definition with the vocabulary word. Put your answers in the magic squares below. When your answers are correct, all columns and rows will add to the same number.

A. DISHEVELED
B. CHIVALROUS
C. INDIGNANTLY
D. PANTOMIME
E. UNPERTURBED
F. MANIPULATES
G. SWADDLED
H. UNOBSTRUCTED
I. DEFERENTIAL
J. PAROXYSM
K. CARICATURE
L. EMPHATIC
M. PRIMER
N. JOVIAL
O. HAGGARD
P. COMPELLED

1. Care worn; drawn
2. Fit; attack
3. In open view
4. Rumpled; untidy
5. Gestures without voice
6. Undisturbed; unbothered
7. Exaggerated model
8. Jolly; happy
9. Maneuvers; moves
10. Righteously angry
11. Manual; handbook
12. Pointed; insistent
13. Respectful; obedient
14. Obliged; made responsible
15. Gentlemanly; gallant
16. Wrapped up

A=	B=	C=	D=
E=	F=	G=	H=
I=	J=	K=	L=
M=	N=	O=	P=

Miracle Worker Vocabulary Magic Squares 2 Answer Key

Match the definition with the vocabulary word. Put your answers in the magic squares below. When your answers are correct, all columns and rows will add to the same number.

A. DISHEVELED
B. CHIVALROUS
C. INDIGNANTLY
D. PANTOMIME
E. UNPERTURBED
F. MANIPULATES
G. SWADDLED
H. UNOBSTRUCTED
I. DEFERENTIAL
J. PAROXYSM
K. CARICATURE
L. EMPHATIC
M. PRIMER
N. JOVIAL
O. HAGGARD
P. COMPELLED

1. Care worn; drawn
2. Fit; attack
3. In open view
4. Rumpled; untidy
5. Gestures without voice
6. Undisturbed; unbothered
7. Exaggerated model
8. Jolly; happy
9. Maneuvers; moves
10. Righteously angry
11. Manual; handbook
12. Pointed; insistent
13. Respectful; obedient
14. Obliged; made responsible
15. Gentlemanly; gallant
16. Wrapped up

A=4	B=15	C=10	D=5
E=6	F=9	G=16	H=3
I=13	J=2	K=7	L=12
M=11	N=8	O=1	P=14

Miracle Worker Vocabulary Magic Squares 3

Match the definition with the vocabulary word. Put your answers in the magic squares below. When your answers are correct, all columns and rows will add to the same number.

A. DEPRIVATION
B. PRIMER
C. AFFLICTION
D. COMPELLED
E. APPRAISAL
F. PROFFERED
G. TREPIDATION
H. DEFERENTIAL
I. NETTLED
J. UNPERTURBED
K. OMINOUSLY
L. VIGIL
M. PAROXYSM
N. ALMSHOUSE
O. AVERSION
P. PUMMELS

1. Loss
2. Sanitarium
3. Undisturbed; unbothered
4. Evaluation
5. Fear; alarm
6. A watch
7. Thrashes; beats
8. Hardship; problem
9. Distaste for; dislike for
10. Obliged; made responsible
11. Respectful; obedient
12. Threateningly; darkly; gloomily
13. Bothered; peeved
14. Offered forth
15. Manual; handbook
16. Fit; attack

A=	B=	C=	D=
E=	F=	G=	H=
I=	J=	K=	L=
M=	N=	O=	P=

Miracle Worker Vocabulary Magic Squares 3 Answer Key

Match the definition with the vocabulary word. Put your answers in the magic squares below. When your answers are correct, all columns and rows will add to the same number.

A. DEPRIVATION
B. PRIMER
C. AFFLICTION
D. COMPELLED
E. APPRAISAL
F. PROFFERED
G. TREPIDATION
H. DEFERENTIAL
I. NETTLED
J. UNPERTURBED
K. OMINOUSLY
L. VIGIL
M. PAROXYSM
N. ALMSHOUSE
O. AVERSION
P. PUMMELS

1. Loss
2. Sanitarium
3. Undisturbed; unbothered
4. Evaluation
5. Fear; alarm
6. A watch
7. Thrashes; beats
8. Hardship; problem
9. Distaste for; dislike for
10. Obliged; made responsible
11. Respectful; obedient
12. Threateningly; darkly; gloomily
13. Bothered; peeved
14. Offered forth
15. Manual; handbook
16. Fit; attack

A=1	B=15	C=8	D=10
E=4	F=14	G=5	H=11
I=13	J=3	K=12	L=6
M=16	N=2	O=9	P=7

Miracle Worker Vocabulary Magic Squares 4

Match the definition with the vocabulary word. Put your answers in the magic squares below. When your answers are correct, all columns and rows will add to the same number.

A. DISENGAGE
B. AVERSION
C. PANTOMIME
D. INTRACTABLY
E. TYRANT
F. IMPERIOUS
G. RESOLUTELY
H. JOVIAL
I. IMPERTINENT
J. TREPIDATION
K. MANIPULATES
L. DEFERENTIAL
M. FORLORN
N. EMPHATIC
O. FACETIOUSLY
P. OBSTINATE

1. Flippant; smart-alecky
2. Inflexibly; in a headstrong manner
3. Fear; alarm
4. Harsh, cruel leader
5. Rude; impolite
6. Urgent; pressing
7. Stubborn; headstrong
8. Gestures without voice
9. Jolly; happy
10. Maneuvers; moves
11. Release; undo
12. Pointed; insistent
13. Distaste for; dislike for
14. Forsaken; abandoned
15. Deliberately; willfully
16. Respectful; obedient

A=	B=	C=	D=
E=	F=	G=	H=
I=	J=	K=	L=
M=	N=	O=	P=

Miracle Worker Vocabulary Magic Squares 4 Answer Key

Match the definition with the vocabulary word. Put your answers in the magic squares below. When your answers are correct, all columns and rows will add to the same number.

A. DISENGAGE
B. AVERSION
C. PANTOMIME
D. INTRACTABLY
E. TYRANT
F. IMPERIOUS
G. RESOLUTELY
H. JOVIAL
I. IMPERTINENT
J. TREPIDATION
K. MANIPULATES
L. DEFERENTIAL
M. FORLORN
N. EMPHATIC
O. FACETIOUSLY
P. OBSTINATE

1. Flippant; smart-alecky
2. Inflexibly; in a headstrong manner
3. Fear; alarm
4. Harsh, cruel leader
5. Rude; impolite
6. Urgent; pressing
7. Stubborn; headstrong
8. Gestures without voice
9. Jolly; happy
10. Maneuvers; moves
11. Release; undo
12. Pointed; insistent
13. Distaste for; dislike for
14. Forsaken; abandoned
15. Deliberately; willfully
16. Respectful; obedient

A=11	B=13	C=8	D=2
E=4	F=6	G=15	H=9
I=5	J=3	K=10	L=16
M=14	N=12	O=1	P=7

Miracle Worker Vocabulary Word Search 1

```
I N I T D U N P E R T U R B E D I G E J
R O N Y I P E A D M D C F V O N N R G B
R N E R S U T R U H W J I U T I U T A T
E P X A H M T O T D B T R I R T C E G L
S L O N E L X I Q U L M E A W O M N H
O U R T V E E Y C N Y A H C C R M P E C
L S A X E L D S I J T T I L H I P S R
U E B Z L S M L I I R K V O T E R I D
T D L F E C I B O W A C F H M H L A D F
E E Y V D D L N S C I H O O A E L N V W
V X S W E H S J J T I I C M R S E C J Y
I I Y W J X Q J A W M V U Z B L D E L S
M F V Y A V E H H O P A L S Q A O E R A
P S T A Q D P D R P E L I R Y X T R M I
A N B K C M D O L N R S S H U D I N H
S A V L E I S L G Y I O T C L E A D V S
S R A F A E O I E S O U F O L B O G T E
I T L J L N U R D U S S F L L C V S P
V D I Y O E D E S N S E F Y E X N T D H
E P A K B V M L K S R A L N D R N F Z J
L G N C F I I E Y N B K T G Y E E H G G
Y X T Z R T M A E S U O H S M L A D D W
L H L P V P T Y L B A T C A R T N I T C
V X Y Q T S U O N I M U L O V I G I L G
```

A watch (5)
Agreeably; willingly (7)
Allusions; hints (11)
Bewildered; puzzled (9)
Bothered; peeved (7)
Bravely; courageously (9)
Bulky; large (10)
Concern (10)
Confused; bewildered (7)
Deliberately; willfully (10)
Disorderly; messy (7)
Drearily (6)
Exaggerated model (10)
Eye doctor (7)
Favorable; harmless (6)
Fit; attack (8)
Flatly; tritely (7)
Forsaken; abandoned (7)
Gentlemanly; gallant (10)
Gloomily; sullenly (8)
Harsh, cruel leader (6)
Idle; inactive (8)
Inclined to fight (9)
Inflammation of the eyelids (8)

Inflexibly; in a headstrong manner (11)
Irritatedly (7)
Jolly; happy (6)
Lively; spirited (9)
Manual; handbook (6)
Moans; wails (7)
Moderation (10)
Motionless; frozen (10)
Obliged; made responsible (9)
Offered forth (9)
Pointed; insistent (8)
Release; undo (9)
Relentlessly; unyielding (10)
Rumpled; untidy (10)
Sanitarium (9)
Shrinking (9)
Small (10)
Thrashes; beats (7)
Twists from pain; flails (7)
Uncertain; hesitant (10)
Undisturbed; unbothered (11)
Unemotionally (11)
Urgent; pressing (9)
Wrapped up (8)

Miracle Worker Vocabulary Word Search 1 Answer Key

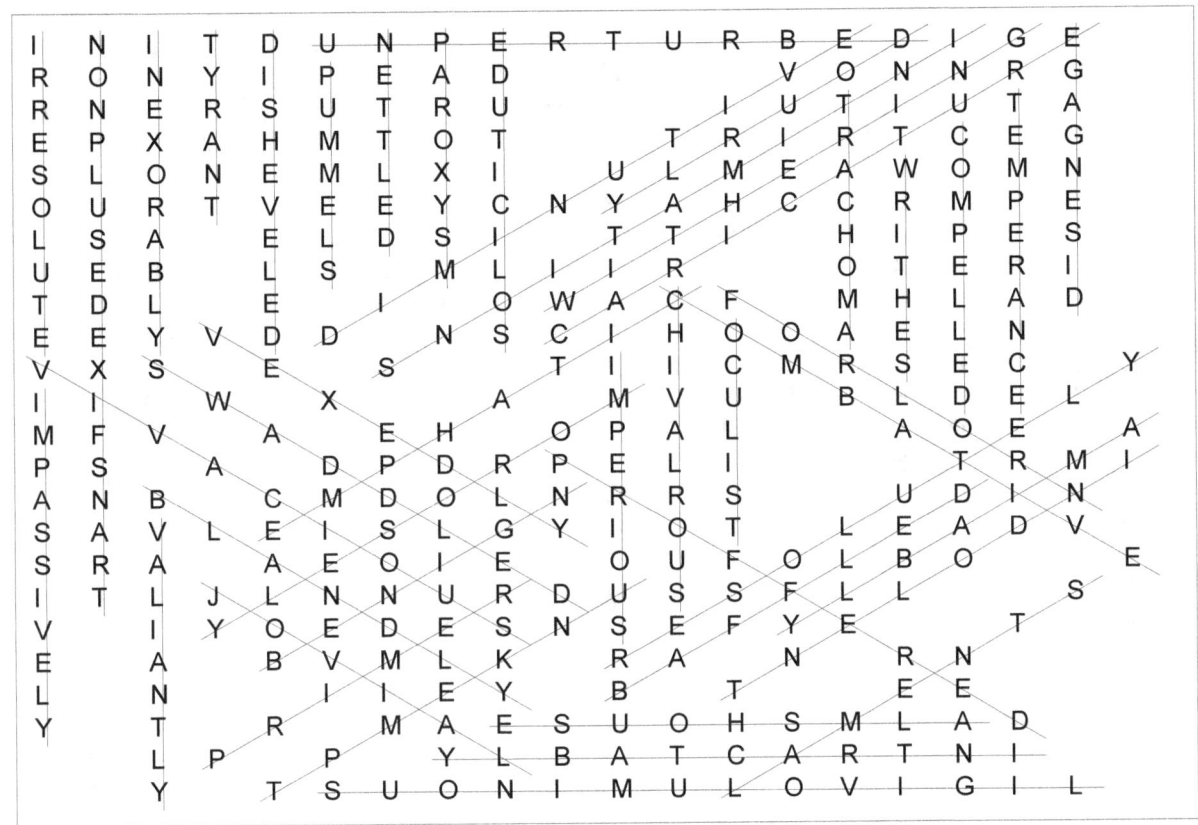

A watch (5)
Agreeably; willingly (7)
Allusions; hints (11)
Bewildered; puzzled (9)
Bothered; peeved (7)
Bravely; courageously (9)
Bulky; large (10)
Concern (10)
Confused; bewildered (7)
Deliberately; willfully (10)
Disorderly; messy (7)
Drearily (6)
Exaggerated model (10)
Eye doctor (7)
Favorable; harmless (6)
Fit; attack (8)
Flatly; tritely (7)
Forsaken; abandoned (7)
Gentlemanly; gallant (10)
Gloomily; sullenly (8)
Harsh, cruel leader (6)
Idle; inactive (8)
Inclined to fight (9)
Inflammation of the eyelids (8)

Inflexibly; in a headstrong manner (11)
Irritatedly (7)
Jolly; happy (6)
Lively; spirited (9)
Manual; handbook (6)
Moans; wails (7)
Moderation (10)
Motionless; frozen (10)
Obliged; made responsible (9)
Offered forth (9)
Pointed; insistent (8)
Release; undo (9)
Relentlessly; unyielding (10)
Rumpled; untidy (10)
Sanitarium (9)
Shrinking (9)
Small (10)
Thrashes; beats (7)
Twists from pain; flails (7)
Uncertain; hesitant (10)
Undisturbed; unbothered (11)
Unemotionally (11)
Urgent; pressing (9)
Wrapped up (8)

Miracle Worker Vocabulary Word Search 2

```
I  N  E  F  F  E  C  T  U  A  L  V  A  L  I  A  N  T  L  Y
I  M  V  R  T  X  C  K  T  F  M  E  P  K  M  P  E  F  U  C
N  N  P  E  L  Z  R  D  N  A  M  R  Y  P  P  T  T  N  P  B
D  I  T  U  X  Z  W  P  C  L  N  I  O  L  E  R  T  V  P  F
I  N  J  I  D  E  D  W  P  I  I  M  F  B  R  A  L  T  E  K
G  A  K  P  M  E  D  Q  L  C  P  O  F  A  I  I  E  R  R  K
N  R  D  U  Z  A  N  L  O  T  U  T  E  T  O  S  D  C  T  F
A  T  X  M  H  K  T  C  Y  I  L  N  R  C  U  A  T  T  U  M
N  I  G  M  K  N  U  I  E  O  A  A  E  A  S  L  Y  Y  R  L
T  C  G  E  W  L  F  B  O  N  T  P  D  R  C  R  S  Z  B  G
L  U  A  L  I  J  I  R  C  N  E  Q  D  T  A  H  U  S  E  C
Y  L  E  S  O  R  O  M  Y  L  S  U  O  N  I  M  O  U  D  V
H  A  T  H  P  Q  C  T  P  T  L  B  T  I  S  L  N  M  K  R
L  T  F  F  B  E  T  O  N  A  S  R  W  V  I  A  I  A  A  M
W  E  S  E  O  Y  R  E  M  T  S  Y  H  C  V  A  M  L  I  H
I  R  P  V  Q  R  M  I  I  P  L  S  I  A  G  M  U  M  N  C
T  B  I  I  J  A  L  N  T  D  E  T  I  N  M  I  L  S  D  P
H  T  N  T  L  V  A  O  N  Y  U  L  I  V  K  A  O  H  O  P
E  P  S  U  H  T  Z  A  R  D  I  T  L  Y  E  B  V  O  L  F
R  R  T  N  E  E  L  G  E  N  A  D  A  E  R  L  R  U  E  R
I  I  E  I  Z  B  S  Y  G  C  D  D  I  V  D  Y  Y  S  N  J
N  M  R  M  H  A  G  G  A  R  D  P  V  J  P  V  S  E  T  N
G  E  V  I  G  I  L  L  Y  L  R  U  O  D  B  E  N  I  G  N
G  R  H  D  E  M  P  H  A  T  I  C  J  U  N  K  E  M  P  T
```

A watch (5)
Agreeably; willingly (7)
Allusions; hints (11)
Boldness (9)
Bothered; peeved (7)
Bravely; courageously (9)
Bulky; large (10)
Care worn; drawn (7)
Concern (10)
Disorderly; messy (7)
Drearily (6)
Evaluation (9)
Eye doctor (7)
Favorable; harmless (6)
Flatly; tritely (7)
Forsaken; abandoned (7)
Gestures without voice (9)
Gloomily; sullenly (8)
Hardship; problem (10)
Harsh, cruel leader (6)
Hopeless; futile (10)
Idle; inactive (8)
Inflammation of the eyelids (8)
Inflexibly; in a headstrong manner (11)

Irritatedly (7)
Jolly; happy (6)
Maneuvers; moves (11)
Manual; handbook (6)
Moans; wails (7)
Obliged; made responsible (9)
Offered forth (9)
Old, unmarried woman (8)
Pointed; insistent (8)
Righteously angry (11)
Sanitarium (9)
Satisfying; gratifying (9)
Shrinking (9)
Small (10)
Somewhat ill-tempered (8)
Stubborn; headstrong (9)
Thrashes; beats (7)
Threateningly; darkly; gloomily (9)
Twists from pain; flails (7)
Undisturbed; unbothered (11)
Unemotionally (11)
Urgent; pressing (9)
Useless (11)
Wordless; silent (12)

Miracle Worker Vocabulary Word Search 2 Answer Key

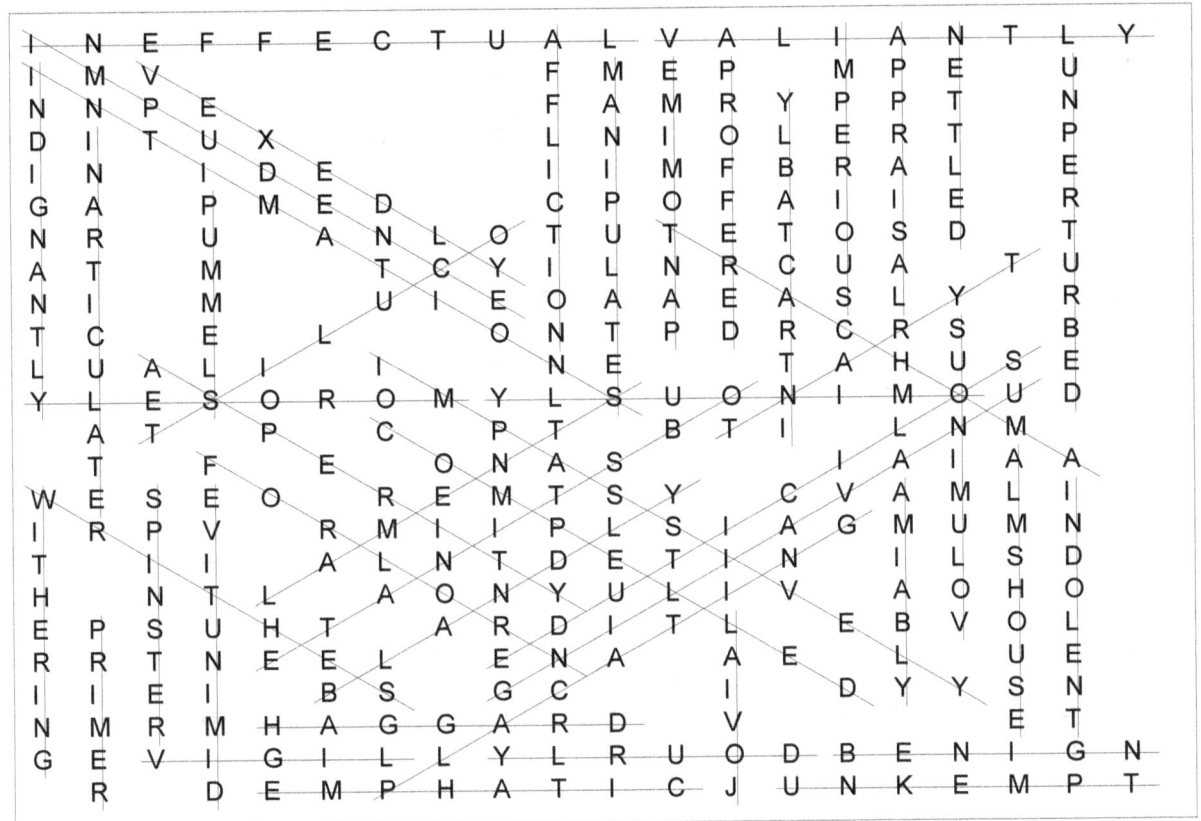

A watch (5)
Agreeably; willingly (7)
Allusions; hints (11)
Boldness (9)
Bothered; peeved (7)
Bravely; courageously (9)
Bulky; large (10)
Care worn; drawn (7)
Concern (10)
Disorderly; messy (7)
Drearily (6)
Evaluation (9)
Eye doctor (7)
Favorable; harmless (6)
Flatly; tritely (7)
Forsaken; abandoned (7)
Gestures without voice (9)
Gloomily; sullenly (8)
Hardship; problem (10)
Harsh, cruel leader (6)
Hopeless; futile (10)
Idle; inactive (8)
Inflammation of the eyelids (8)
Inflexibly; in a headstrong manner (11)

Irritatedly (7)
Jolly; happy (6)
Maneuvers; moves (11)
Manual; handbook (6)
Moans; wails (7)
Obliged; made responsible (9)
Offered forth (9)
Old, unmarried woman (8)
Pointed; insistent (8)
Righteously angry (11)
Sanitarium (9)
Satisfying; gratifying (9)
Shrinking (9)
Small (10)
Somewhat ill-tempered (8)
Stubborn; headstrong (9)
Thrashes; beats (7)
Threateningly; darkly; gloomily (9)
Twists from pain; flails (7)
Undisturbed; unbothered (11)
Unemotionally (11)
Urgent; pressing (9)
Useless (11)
Wordless; silent (12)

Miracle Worker Vocabulary Word Search 3

```
D E P R I V A T I O N I N D U L G E N T
E I Y C D Q C M L A S I A R P P A O P S
L J N T S I O B J T P M E K N U I Q E F
D H D D G R S G N E T T L E D T Z T N C
D S E S O P R E T N I R A G C X A E I K
A N R S D L M C N Y S A L I Q L T T S P
W J E T J A E R H G N Q L V U H A A S L
S L F V L L E N C I A F G P E H E L E R
Y H F Y J M H L T H F G I Q P R L U N R
I I O H I S K S M A I N E M U P S C T X
P M R R L H B Y O I A V E T L Y D I U F
U P A A R O X Y S M B L A N D L Y T O G
M E A U K U V F E P I C C L S R Z R V N
M R N P D S S Y C E I N B S R U L A E H
E I T Y J E L H N R I T O M H O T N D V
L O O Q H B N M A C B N R U R D U I V H
S U M T A A V C R E E A E N S Q M S E C
H S I I G F I D E P N R T X J L W N X K
K R M C G F G V P T I Y S B O H Y K E V
W A E S A L I F M I G T N J V R Q B D Y
X F Y W R E L L E B N Y I G I P A V L J
G C H J D D X Y T L C K P Z A H V B Y V
O C U L I S T X Q Y R E S O L U T E L Y
C O M P U N C T I O N O N P L U S E D Y
```

AFFLICTION	COMPUNCTION	IMPUDENCE	NETTLED	RESOLUTELY
ALMSHOUSE	DEPRIVATION	INARTICULATE	NONPLUSED	SPINSTER
AMIABLY	DEVOUTNESS	INDOLENT	OBSTINATE	SWADDLED
APPRAISAL	DISENGAGE	INDULGENT	OCULIST	TEMPERANCE
AVERSION	DOURLY	INEXORABLY	OMINOUSLY	TYRANT
BAFFLED	EMPHATIC	INTERPOSES	PANTOMIME	UNKEMPT
BENIGN	FORLORN	JOVIAL	PAROXYSM	VEXEDLY
BLANDLY	HAGGARD	LAMENTS	PRIMER	VIGIL
CARICATURE	IMPERCEPTIBLY	MANIPULATES	PROFFERED	WRITHES
CHIVALROUS	IMPERIOUS	MOROSELY	PUMMELS	

Miracle Worker Vocabulary Word Search 3 Answer Key

AFFLICTION	COMPUNCTION	IMPUDENCE	NETTLED	RESOLUTELY
ALMSHOUSE	DEPRIVATION	INARTICULATE	NONPLUSED	SPINSTER
AMIABLY	DEVOUTNESS	INDOLENT	OBSTINATE	SWADDLED
APPRAISAL	DISENGAGE	INDULGENT	OCULIST	TEMPERANCE
AVERSION	DOURLY	INEXORABLY	OMINOUSLY	TYRANT
BAFFLED	EMPHATIC	INTERPOSES	PANTOMIME	UNKEMPT
BENIGN	FORLORN	JOVIAL	PAROXYSM	VEXEDLY
BLANDLY	HAGGARD	LAMENTS	PRIMER	VIGIL
CARICATURE	IMPERCEPTIBLY	MANIPULATES	PROFFERED	WRITHES
CHIVALROUS	IMPERIOUS	MOROSELY	PUMMELS	

Miracle Worker Vocabulary Word Search 4

```
U N A V A I L I N G P A N T O M I M E D
N G I N E B E M P H A T I C C G Y R L G
P T P P Z L V W K R R K H V H P U X B R
E G A V H B I R T C O H L F Q T J H A C
R P L A C A T I N G X F V P A L D Z N L
T D M L N F A T E D Y V F C N E F Y I D
U M S I B F B H L G S Q I E C P R L M S
R Z H A T L M E O B M R V N R M F B R M
B Q O N R E O S D R A S E I D E Z I E L
E P U T E D C E N C N M M R Q V D T T Q
D U S L P D L X I O M E A Y C O F P N Q
B M E Y I D N X I O R G E B Q L A E I C
D M L R D T R T C L G T L F Z U C C T Y
D E N A A N A E T A A A T L W M E R M B
A L W L T M R T H L N M N N P I T E F W
N S O L I C I T U D E R E T S N I P S V
E T P T O N Y C L M W T G N G O O M U P
T G N E N L I Y O R A V L A T U U I O Z
T I N R R T Y R A N T I U M P S S J L S
L T F U R I O B I G H G D I M Z L O O M
E S O A Y S T T D X S I N A E Q Y V V G
D D N Y E Z S Y X C K L I B K C C I I M
G I H L J B F O R L O R N L N S H A R V
X W Y M O C U L I S T M Y Y U D Q L F B
```

ALMSHOUSE	EMPHATIC	INTERMINABLE	PAROXYSM	TREPIDATION
AMIABLY	FACETIOUSLY	INTIMATIONS	PLACATING	TYRANT
ASPERITY	FORLORN	JOVIAL	PRIMER	UNAVAILING
BAFFLED	FRIVOLOUS	LAMENTS	PROFFERED	UNKEMPT
BENIGN	HAGGARD	MOROSELY	PUMMELS	UNPERTURBED
BLANDLY	IMPERCEPTIBLY	NETTLED	RECOMMENCED	VALIANTLY
CARICATURE	INARTICULATE	OBSTINATE	SOLICITUDE	VIGIL
COMBATIVE	INDOLENT	OCULIST	SPINSTER	VOLUMINOUS
DOURLY	INDULGENT	PANTOMIME	SWADDLED	WRITHES

Miracle Worker Vocabulary Word Search 4 Answer Key

```
U   N   A   V   A   I   L   I   N   G   P   A   N   T   O   M   I   M   E
N   G   I   N   E   B   E   M   P   H   A   T   I   C       R   L
P               V   W       R   R                   U       B
E       A   V       B   I   T   T           T       T       A
R   P   L   A   C   A   T   I   N   G   X   F       A   D       N
T       M   L       F   A   T   E   O       F   C   E       Y   I
U       S   I       F   B   H   L   S       I   E   P       L   M
R       H   A   T   L   M   E   O       M   R   N       B   I   R
B       O   N   R   E   E   S   D       A   S   E   I   D   E   T
E   P   U   T   E   D   O   E       C   N   M   R   V       T   N
D   U   S   L   P           L       O   M   E       O   F   P   I
    M   E   Y   I           T       I   O   G       L   A   E
    M       A   D       T       E   A   G   T       U   C   R
    E           T   E   A   E   A   N       M   E   T
A   L   W   A   M   R       H   L   N   M       N   I   P
N   S   O   L   I   C   I   T   U   D   E   R   T   S   N   I   P   S
E       P   T   O       C   L   M       T   G   N   O   O   M   U
T       N   E   N   L   I   Y   O       A   V   L   A   T   U   I   O
T   I           R   T   Y   R   A   N   T   I   U   M   P   S   J   O
L               U   R   I   O       I       G   D       M   L   O   V
E       O   A       S   T   T       L       I   N   A   E   I   V
D   D   N       E       S   Y       N   I   N   B   K       I   R
    I           L       B   F   O   R   L   O   R   N   L   A   R
    Y           O   C   U   L   I   S   T           Y   U   L   F
```

ALMSHOUSE	EMPHATIC	INTERMINABLE	PAROXYSM	TREPIDATION
AMIABLY	FACETIOUSLY	INTIMATIONS	PLACATING	TYRANT
ASPERITY	FORLORN	JOVIAL	PRIMER	UNAVAILING
BAFFLED	FRIVOLOUS	LAMENTS	PROFFERED	UNKEMPT
BENIGN	HAGGARD	MOROSELY	PUMMELS	UNPERTURBED
BLANDLY	IMPERCEPTIBLY	NETTLED	RECOMMENCED	VALIANTLY
CARICATURE	INARTICULATE	OBSTINATE	SOLICITUDE	VIGIL
COMBATIVE	INDOLENT	OCULIST	SPINSTER	VOLUMINOUS
DOURLY	INDULGENT	PANTOMIME	SWADDLED	WRITHES

Miracle Worker Vocabulary Crossword 1

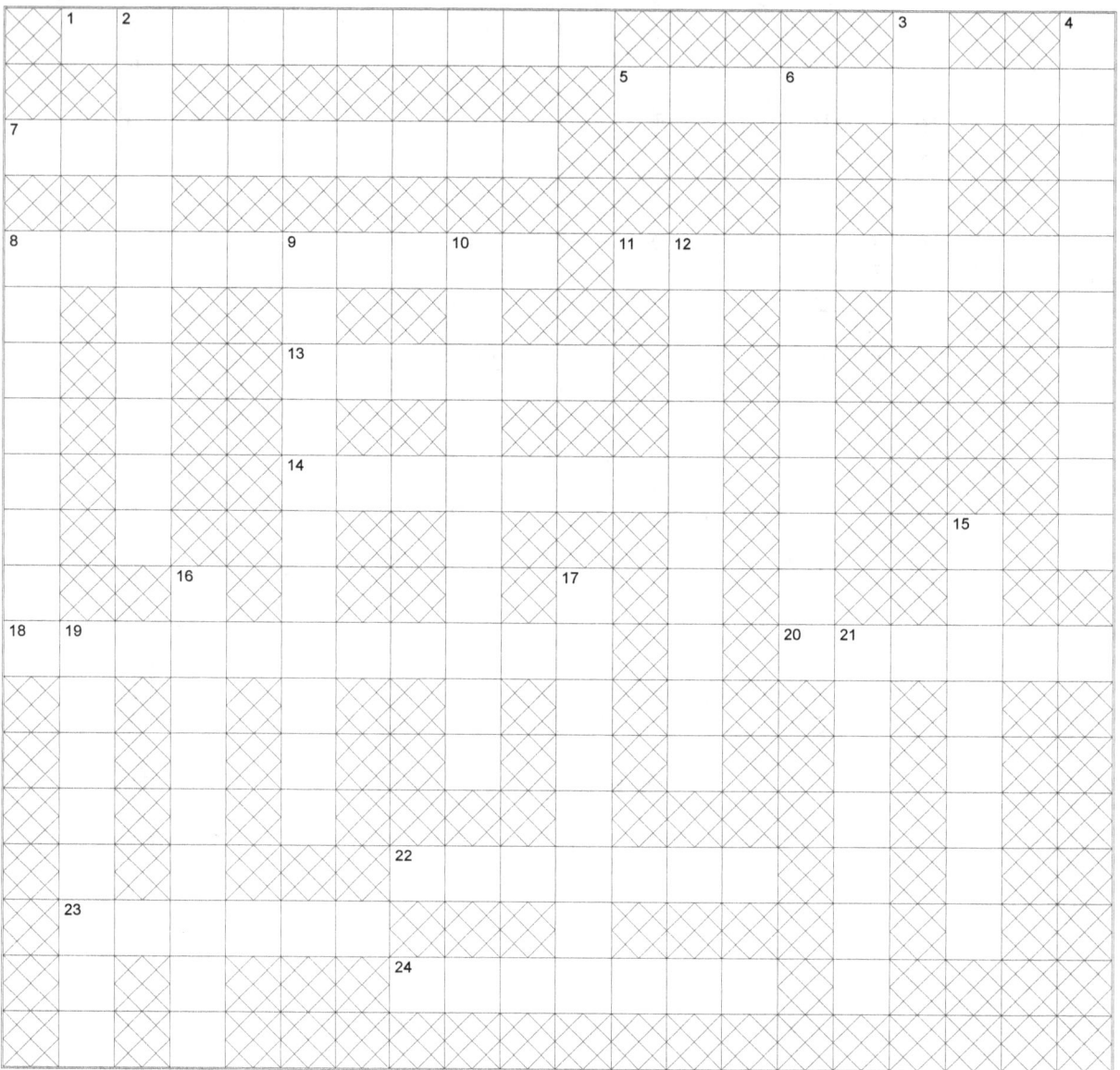

Across
1. Motionless; frozen
5. Boldness
7. Rumpled; untidy
8. Concern
11. Release; undo
13. Manual; handbook
14. Old, unmarried woman
18. Loss
20. Drearily
22. Disorderly; messy
23. Harsh, cruel leader
24. Twists from pain; flails

Down
2. Deliberately; willfully
3. Favorable; harmless
4. Moderation
6. Undisturbed; unbothered
8. Wrapped up
9. Unemotionally
10. Small
12. Intervenes; interferes
15. Gloomily; sullenly
16. Offered forth
17. Idle; inactive
19. Pointed; insistent
21. Eye doctor

Miracle Worker Vocabulary Crossword 1 Answer Key

Across
1. Motionless; frozen — TRANSFIXED
5. Boldness — IMPUDENCE
7. Rumpled; untidy — DISHEVELED
8. Concern — SOLICITUDE
11. Release; undo — DISENGAGE
13. Manual; handbook — PRIMER
14. Old, unmarried woman — SPINSTER
18. Loss — DEPRIVATION
20. Drearily — DOURLY
22. Disorderly; messy — UNKEMPT
23. Harsh, cruel leader — TYRANT
24. Twists from pain; flails — WRITHES

Down
2. Deliberately; willfully — RESOLUTELY
3. Favorable; harmless — BENIGN
4. Moderation — TEMPERANCE
6. Undisturbed; unbothered — UNINJURED (UNPINIBED?)
8. Wrapped up — SWADDLED
9. Unemotionally — IMPASSIVELY
10. Small — DIMINUTIVE
12. Intervenes; interferes — INTERRUPTS
15. Gloomily; sullenly — MOROSELY
16. Offered forth — PROFFERED
17. Idle; inactive — INDISPOSED
19. Pointed; insistent — EMPHATIC
21. Eye doctor — OCULIST

Miracle Worker Vocabulary Crossword 2

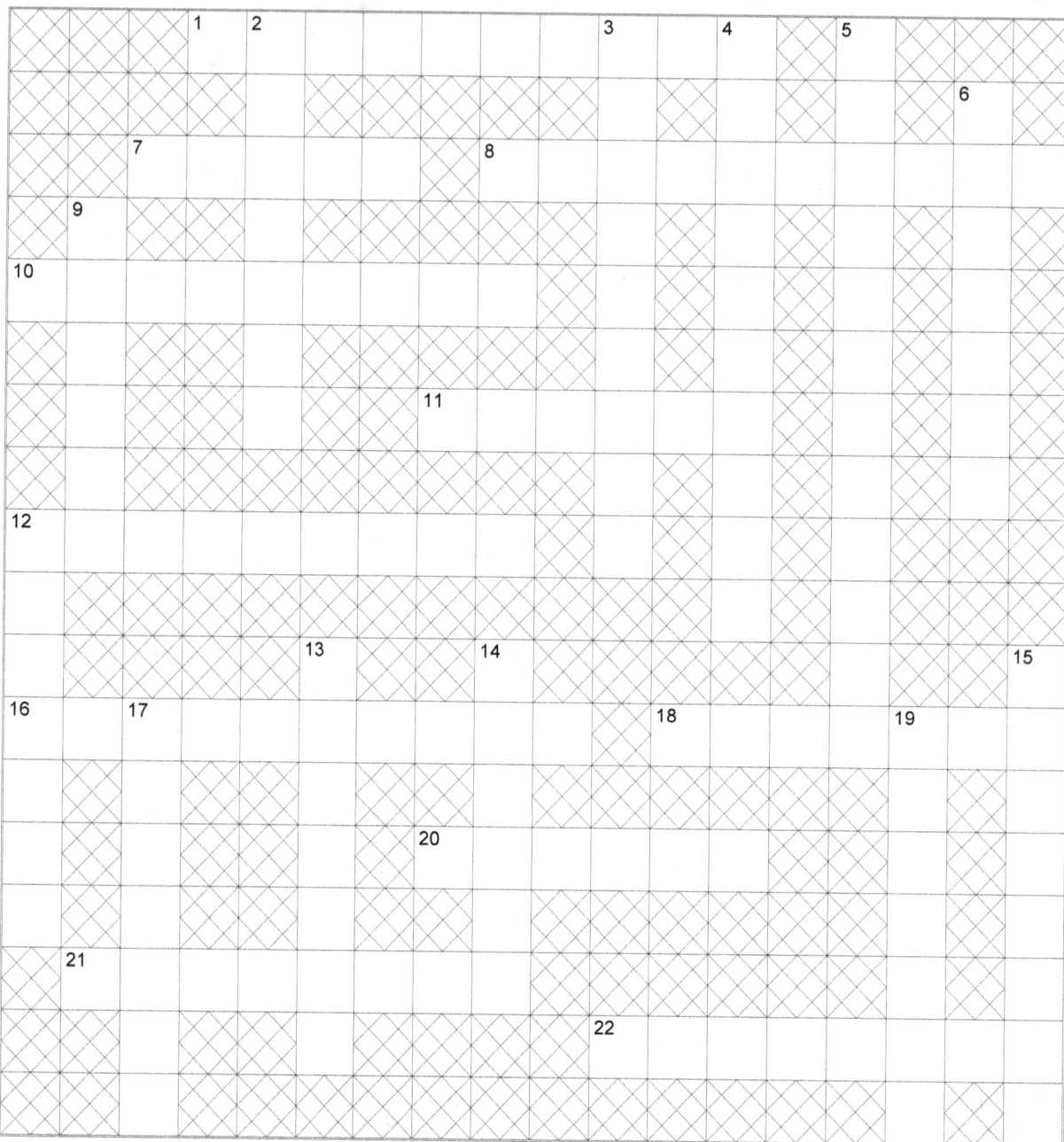

Across
1. Gentlemanly; gallant
7. A watch
8. Deliberately; willfully
10. Inclined to fight
11. Harsh, cruel leader
12. Sanitarium
16. Hardship; problem
18. Moans; wails
20. Manual; handbook
21. Gloomily; sullenly
22. Idle; inactive

Down
2. Care worn; drawn
3. Stubborn; headstrong
4. Concern
5. Unending; ceaseless
6. Flatly; tritely
9. Jolly; happy
12. Agreeably; willingly
13. Eye doctor
14. Drearily
15. Somewhat ill-tempered
17. Forsaken; abandoned
19. Bothered; peeved

Miracle Worker Vocabulary Crossword 2 Answer Key

Across
1. Gentlemanly; gallant
7. A watch
8. Deliberately; willfully
10. Inclined to fight
11. Harsh, cruel leader
12. Sanitarium
16. Hardship; problem
18. Moans; wails
20. Manual; handbook
21. Gloomily; sullenly
22. Idle; inactive

Down
2. Care worn; drawn
3. Stubborn; headstrong
4. Concern
5. Unending; ceaseless
6. Flatly; tritely
9. Jolly; happy
12. Agreeably; willingly
13. Eye doctor
14. Drearily
15. Somewhat ill-tempered
17. Forsaken; abandoned
19. Bothered; peeved

Miracle Worker Vocabulary Crossword 3

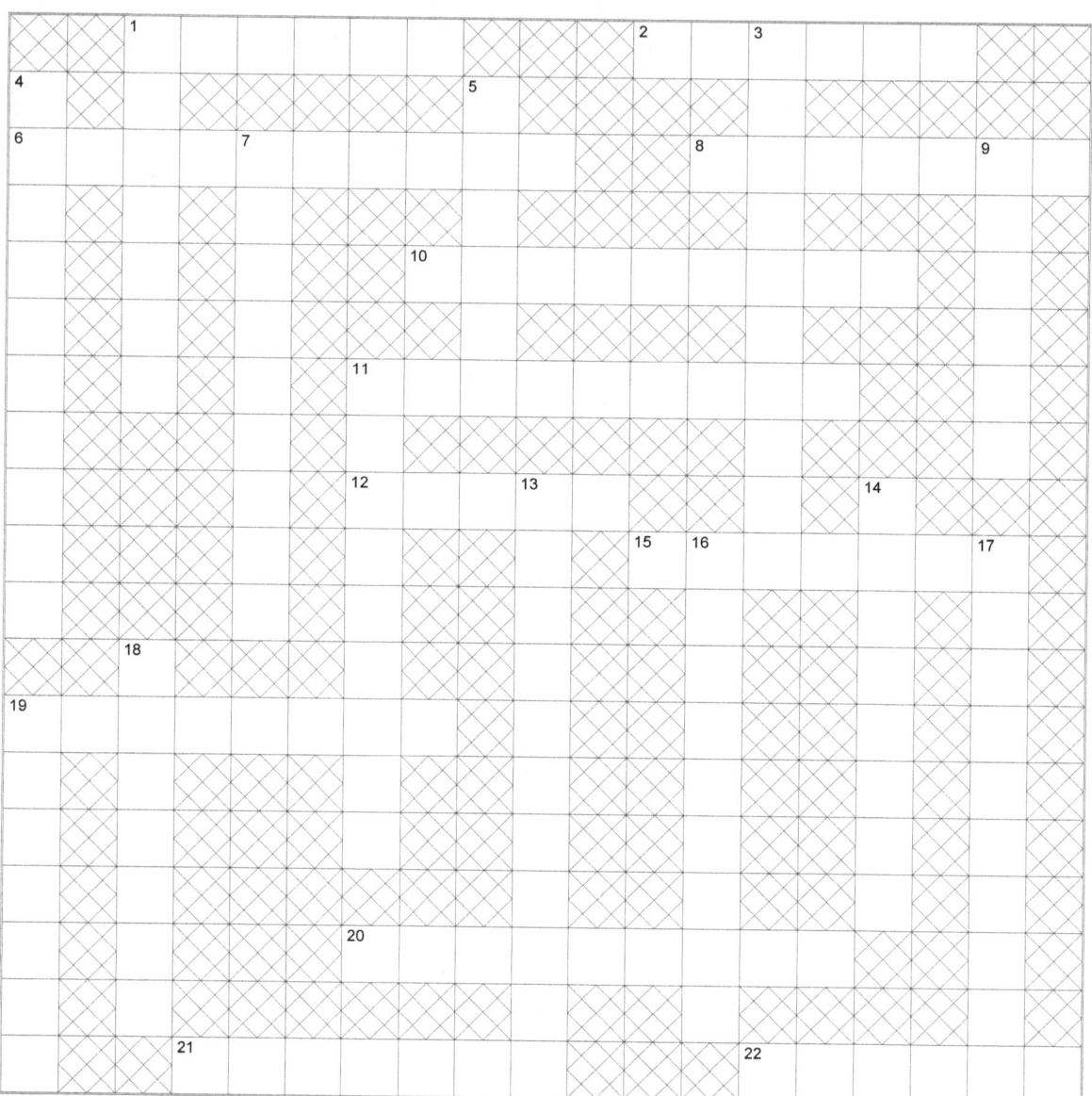

Across
1. Favorable; harmless
2. Drearily
6. Hardship; problem
8. Moans; wails
10. Release; undo
11. Bravely; courageously
12. A watch
15. Care worn; drawn
19. Distaste for; dislike for
20. Stubborn; headstrong
21. Flatly; tritely
22. Manual; handbook

Down
1. Confused; bewildered
3. Hopeless; futile
4. Exaggerated model
5. Jolly; happy
7. Boldness
9. Harsh, cruel leader
11. Lively; spirited
13. Righteously angry
14. Fit; attack
16. Evaluation
17. Small
18. Bothered; peeved
19. Agreeably; willingly

Miracle Worker Vocabulary Crossword 3 Answer Key

		¹B	E	N	I	G	N		²D	³O	U	R	L	Y	
⁴C		A					⁵J			N					
⁶A	F	⁷F	L	I	C	T	I	O	N	⁸L	A	M	E	N	⁹T	S
R		F		M			V			V				Y	
I		L		P		¹⁰D	I	S	E	N	G	A	G	E		R
C		E		U			A			I				A	
A		D		D	¹¹V	A	L	I	A	N	T	L	Y		N
T				E		I				T				T
U				N	¹²V	I	G	¹³I	L		N		¹⁴P
R				C		A		N		¹⁵H	¹⁶A	G	G	A	R	¹⁷D
E				E		C		D		P		R		I
		¹⁸N			I		I		P		O		M
¹⁹A	V	E	R	S	I	O	N		G		R		X		I
M		T			U		N		A		Y		N
I		T			S		A		I		S		U
A		L					N		S		M		T
B		E		²⁰O	B	S	T	I	N	A	T	E		I
L		D					L		L				V
Y		²¹B	L	A	N	D	L	Y		²²P	R	I	M	E	R

Across
1. Favorable; harmless
2. Drearily
6. Hardship; problem
8. Moans; wails
10. Release; undo
11. Bravely; courageously
12. A watch
15. Care worn; drawn
19. Distaste for; dislike for
20. Stubborn; headstrong
21. Flatly; tritely
22. Manual; handbook

Down
1. Confused; bewildered
3. Hopeless; futile
4. Exaggerated model
5. Jolly; happy
7. Boldness
9. Harsh, cruel leader
11. Lively; spirited
13. Righteously angry
14. Fit; attack
16. Evaluation
17. Small
18. Bothered; peeved
19. Agreeably; willingly

Miracle Worker Vocabulary Crossword 4

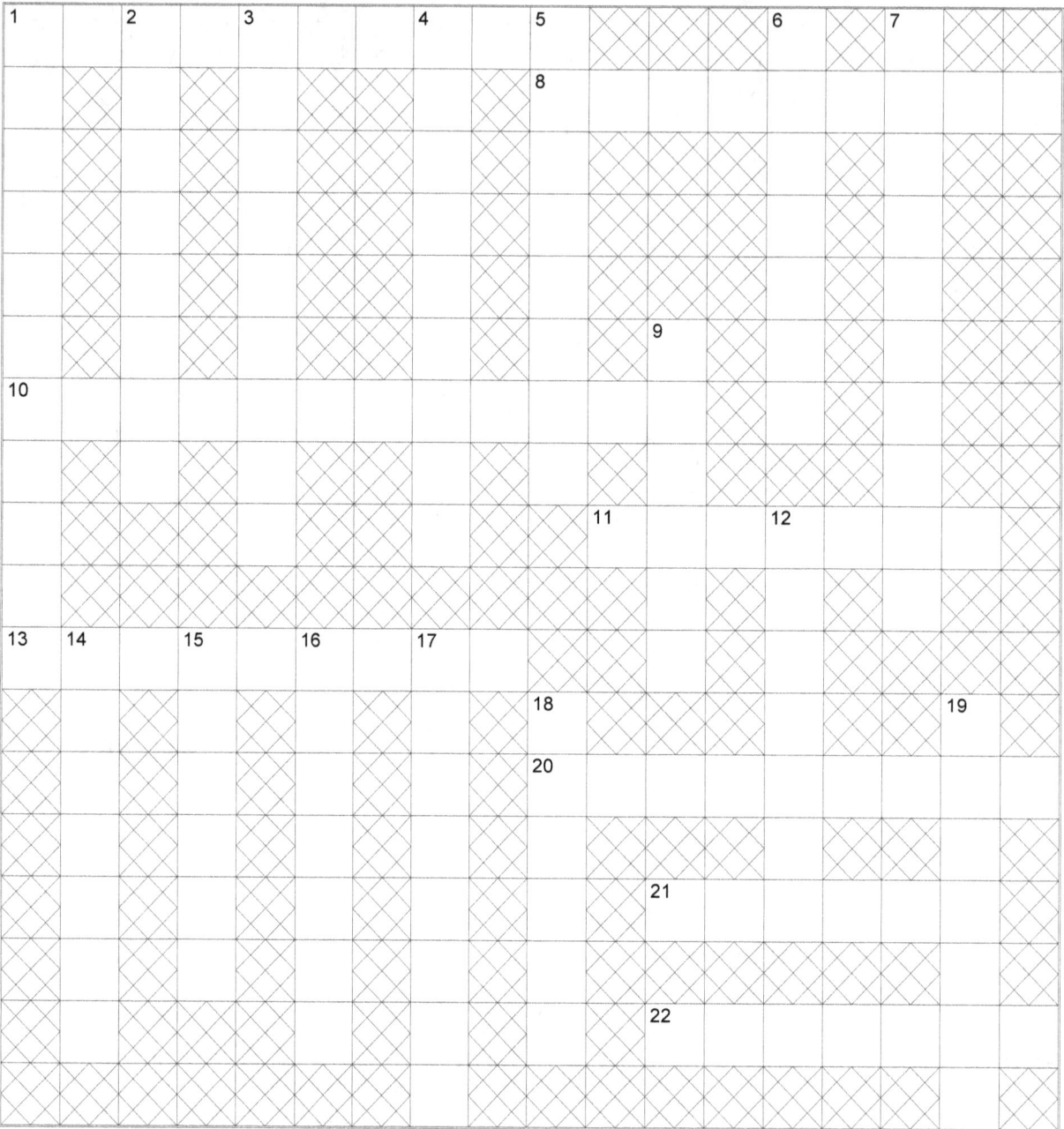

Across
1. Gentlemanly; gallant
8. Shrinking
10. Absolutely; perfectly
11. Confused; bewildered
13. Bewildered; puzzled
20. Threateningly; darkly; gloomily
21. Favorable; harmless
22. Irritatedly

Down
1. Shame; regret
2. Idle; inactive
3. Sanitarium
4. Stubborn; headstrong
5. Wrapped up
6. Bothered; peeved
7. Rumpled; untidy
9. Harsh, cruel leader
12. Forsaken; abandoned
14. Eye doctor
15. Manual; handbook
16. Disorderly; messy
17. Pointed; insistent
18. Jolly; happy
19. Flatly; tritely

Miracle Worker Vocabulary Crossword 4 Answer Key

	1 C	H	2 I	V	3 A	L	R	4 O	U	5 S			6 N		7 D	
	O		N		L			B		8 W	I	T	H	E	R	I	N	G
	M		D		M			S		A			T		S	
	P		O		S			T		D			T		H	
	U		L		H			I		D			L		E	
	N		E		O			N		L		9 T	E		V	
	10 C	O	N	S	U	M	M	A	T	E	L	Y		D		E	
	T		T		S			T		D		R		11		12	
	I				E			E				11 B	A	F	F	L	E	D
	O											N		O		D	
13 N	14 O	N	15 P	L	16 U	S	17 E	D				T		R		
	C		R		N		M		18 J			L		19 B	
	U		I		K		P		20 O	M	I	N	O	U	S	L	Y
	L		M		E		H		V			R		A	
	I		E		M		A		I		21 B	E	N	I	G	N
	S		R		P		T		A					D	
	T				T		I		L		22 V	E	X	E	D	L	Y
							C							Y	

Across
1. Gentlemanly; gallant
8. Shrinking
10. Absolutely; perfectly
11. Confused; bewildered
13. Bewildered; puzzled
20. Threateningly; darkly; gloomily
21. Favorable; harmless
22. Irritatedly

Down
1. Shame; regret
2. Idle; inactive
3. Sanitarium
4. Stubborn; headstrong
5. Wrapped up
6. Bothered; peeved
7. Rumpled; untidy
9. Harsh, cruel leader
12. Forsaken; abandoned
14. Eye doctor
15. Manual; handbook
16. Disorderly; messy
17. Pointed; insistent
18. Jolly; happy
19. Flatly; tritely

Miracle Worker Vocabulary Juggle Letters 1

1. APALSRIAP   = 1. _____
                         Evaluation

2. OCUPTNINMOC   = 2. _____
                         Shame; regret

3. UIYSAOLCTEF   = 3. _____
                         Flippant; smart-alecky

4. ENDLNITO   = 4. _____
                         Idle; inactive

5. ENTTAACIILRU   = 5. _____
                         Wordless; silent

6. NDYLLAB   = 6. _____
                         Flatly; tritely

7. NGNEBI   = 7. _____
                         Favorable; harmless

8. LTEYROEUSL   = 8. _____
                         Deliberately; willfully

9. EFAFLDB   = 9. _____
                         Confused; bewildered

10. TSEANTOIB   =10. _____
                         Stubborn; headstrong

11. YVALIALNT   =11. _____
                         Bravely; courageously

12. MELSNTMOUCAY   =12. _____
                         Absolutely; perfectly

13. NFRROOL   =13. _____
                         Forsaken; abandoned

14. AORACMHT   =14. _____
                         Inflammation of the eyelids

15. ENKPMTU   =15. _____
                         Disorderly; messy

Miracle Worker Vocabulary Juggle Letters 1 Answer Key

1. APALSRIAP = 1. APPARAISAL
Evaluation

2. OCUPTNINMOC = 2. COMPUNCTION
Shame; regret

3. UIYSAOLCTEF = 3. FACETIOUSLY
Flippant; smart-alecky

4. ENDLNITO = 4. INDOLENT
Idle; inactive

5. ENTTAACIILRU = 5. INARTICULATE
Wordless; silent

6. NDYLLAB = 6. BLANDLY
Flatly; tritely

7. NGNEBI = 7. BENIGN
Favorable; harmless

8. LTEYROEUSL = 8. RESOLUTELY
Deliberately; willfully

9. EFAFLDB = 9. BAFFLED
Confused; bewildered

10. TSEANTOIB =10. OBSTINATE
Stubborn; headstrong

11. YVALIALNT =11. VALIANTLY
Bravely; courageously

12. MELSNTMOUCAY =12. CONSUMMATELY
Absolutely; perfectly

13. NFRROOL =13. FORLORN
Forsaken; abandoned

14. AORACMHT =14. TRACHOMA
Inflammation of the eyelids

15. ENKPMTU =15. UNKEMPT
Disorderly; messy

Copyrighted

Miracle Worker Vocabulary Juggle Letters 2

1. IPINEREMNTT = 1. _____
   Rude; impolite

2. NNEOTLID = 2. _____
   Idle; inactive

3. NNTOIMSITAI = 3. _____
   Allusions; hints

4. APYSELMVIIS = 4. _____
   Unemotionally

5. NTGLUINDE = 5. _____
   Permissive; lenient

6. ETMIIDUVIN = 6. _____
   Small

7. VVICUAOSI = 7. _____
   Lively; spirited

8. PMTEECNERA = 8. _____
   Moderation

9. RCRUCAIATE = 9. _____
   Exaggerated model

10. TTSEBOIAN =10. _____
    Stubborn; headstrong

11. LLUOYESERT =11. _____
    Deliberately; willfully

12. XEYAOILNRB =12. _____
    Relentlessly; unyielding

13. GNBEIN =13. _____
    Favorable; harmless

14. EEBWOOEGN =14. _____
    Miserable; sorrowful

15. IOPISMRUE =15. _____
    Urgent; pressing

Miracle Worker Vocabulary Juggle Letters 2 Answer Key

1. IPINEREMNTT = 1. IMPERTINENT
   Rude; impolite

2. NNEOTLID = 2. INDOLENT
   Idle; inactive

3. NNTOIMSITAI = 3. INTIMATIONS
   Allusions; hints

4. APYSELMVIIS = 4. IMPASSIVELY
   Unemotionally

5. NTGLUINDE = 5. INDULGENT
   Permissive; lenient

6. ETMIIDUVIN = 6. DIMINUTIVE
   Small

7. VVICUAOSI = 7. VIVACIOUS
   Lively; spirited

8. PMTEECNERA = 8. TEMPERANCE
   Moderation

9. RCRUCAIATE = 9. CARICATURE
   Exaggerated model

10. TTSEBOIAN = 10. OBSTINATE
    Stubborn; headstrong

11. LLUOYESERT = 11. RESOLUTELY
    Deliberately; willfully

12. XEYAOILNRB = 12. INEXORABLY
    Relentlessly; unyielding

13. GNBEIN = 13. BENIGN
    Favorable; harmless

14. EEBWOOEGN = 14. WOEBEGONE
    Miserable; sorrowful

15. IOPISMRUE = 15. IMPERIOUS
    Urgent; pressing

Miracle Worker Vocabulary Juggle Letters 3

1. QLSEHNEIURIS = 1. _____
   Resigns; gives up

2. TSRELUYELO = 2. _____
   Deliberately; willfully

3. ESOMALHUS = 3. _____
   Sanitarium

4. ADEDWLDS = 4. _____
   Wrapped up

5. SIISYEAPLMV = 5. _____
   Unemotionally

6. TRATYN = 6. _____
   Harsh, cruel leader

7. ELNIFTCAFEU = 7. _____
   Useless

8. LSOMOREY = 8. _____
   Gloomily; sullenly

9. PAERECETNM = 9. _____
   Moderation

10. RATAOHCM =10. _____
    Inflammation of the eyelids

11. GRTHIWNEI =11. _____
    Shrinking

12. EOGEOWNBE =12. _____
    Miserable; sorrowful

13. SOERNPTEIS =13. _____
    Intervenes; interferes

14. TAVYNLLIA =14. _____
    Bravely; courageously

15. AVLJOI =15. _____
    Jolly; happy

Miracle Worker Vocabulary Juggle Letters 3 Answer Key

1. QLSEHNEIURIS = 1. RELINQUISHES
   Resigns; gives up

2. TSRELUYELO = 2. RESOLUTELY
   Deliberately; willfully

3. ESOMALHUS = 3. ALMSHOUSE
   Sanitarium

4. ADEDWLDS = 4. SWADDLED
   Wrapped up

5. SIISYEAPLMV = 5. IMPASSIVELY
   Unemotionally

6. TRATYN = 6. TYRANT
   Harsh, cruel leader

7. ELNIFTCAFEU = 7. INEFFECTUAL
   Useless

8. LSOMOREY = 8. MOROSELY
   Gloomily; sullenly

9. PAERECETNM = 9. TEMPERANCE
   Moderation

10. RATAOHCM =10. TRACHOMA
    Inflammation of the eyelids

11. GRTHIWNEI =11. WITHERING
    Shrinking

12. EOGEOWNBE =12. WOEBEGONE
    Miserable; sorrowful

13. SOERNPTEIS =13. INTERPOSES
    Intervenes; interferes

14. TAVYNLLIA =14. VALIANTLY
    Bravely; courageously

15. AVLJOI =15. JOVIAL
    Jolly; happy

Miracle Worker Vocabulary Juggle Letters 4

1. TWRSIHE = 1. _____
   Twists from pain; flails

2. NGSEIADGE = 2. _____
   Release; undo

3. SEVORIAN = 3. _____
   Distaste for; dislike for

4. MAENMIOTP = 4. _____
   Gestures without voice

5. SOEHUASLM = 5. _____
   Sanitarium

6. SPOELNDNU = 6. _____
   Bewildered; puzzled

7. UVSLIUOMON = 7. _____
   Bulky; large

8. OIUAFEYCSLT = 8. _____
   Flippant; smart-alecky

9. EEOMECNCMRD = 9. _____
   Repeated; began again

10. IFONLTICAF =10. _____
    Hardship; problem

11. UNTDEINLG =11. _____
    Permissive; lenient

12. RYAPXMOS =12. _____
    Fit; attack

13. ILTCUOS =13. _____
    Eye doctor

14. LLEMCPODE =14. _____
    Obliged; made responsible

15. MLSPEUM =15. _____
    Thrashes; beats

Miracle Worker Vocabulary Juggle Letters 4 Answer Key

1. TWRSIHE = 1. WRITHES
Twists from pain; flails

2. NGSEIADGE = 2. DISENGAGE
Release; undo

3. SEVORIAN = 3. AVERSION
Distaste for; dislike for

4. MAENMIOTP = 4. PANTOMIME
Gestures without voice

5. SOEHUASLM = 5. ALMSHOUSE
Sanitarium

6. SPOELNDNU = 6. NONPLUSED
Bewildered; puzzled

7. UVSLIUOMON = 7. VOLUMINOUS
Bulky; large

8. OIUAFEYCSLT = 8. FACETIOUSLY
Flippant; smart-alecky

9. EEOMECNCMRD = 9. RECOMMENCED
Repeated; began again

10. IFONLTICAF =10. AFFLICTION
Hardship; problem

11. UNTDEINLG =11. INDULGENT
Permissive; lenient

12. RYAPXMOS =12. PAROXYSM
Fit; attack

13. ILTCUOS =13. OCULIST
Eye doctor

14. LLEMCPODE =14. COMPELLED
Obliged; made responsible

15. MLSPEUM =15. PUMMELS
Thrashes; beats

AFFLICTION	Hardship; problem
ALMSHOUSE	Sanitarium
AMIABLY	Agreeably; willingly
APPRAISAL	Evaluation
ASPERITY	Somewhat ill-tempered
AVERSION	Distaste for; dislike for

BAFFLED	Confused; bewildered
BENIGN	Favorable; harmless
BLANDLY	Flatly; tritely
CARICATURE	Exaggerated model
CHIVALROUS	Gentlemanly; gallant
COMBATIVE	Inclined to fight

COMPELLED	Obliged; made responsible
COMPUNCTION	Shame; regret
CONSPICUOUSLY	Clearly; obviously
CONSUMMATELY	Absolutely; perfectly
DEFERENTIAL	Respectful; obedient
DEPRIVATION	Loss

DESICCATED	Dried up
DEVOUTNESS	Godliness; piety
DIMINUTIVE	Small
DISENGAGE	Release; undo
DISHEVELED	Rumpled; untidy
DOURLY	Drearily

EMPHATIC	Pointed; insistent
FACETIOUSLY	Flippant; smart-alecky
FORLORN	Forsaken; abandoned
FRIVOLOUS	Trivial; petty
HAGGARD	Care worn; drawn
IMPASSIVELY	Unemotionally

IMPERCEPTIBLY	Unnoticeably; barely
IMPERIOUS	Urgent; pressing
IMPERTINENT	Rude; impolite
IMPUDENCE	Boldness
INARTICULATE	Wordless; silent
INDIGNANTLY	Righteously angry

INDOLENT	Idle; inactive
INDULGENT	Permissive; lenient
INEFFECTUAL	Useless
INEXORABLY	Relentlessly; unyielding
INTERMINABLE	Unending; ceaseless
INTERPOSES	Intervenes; interferes

INTIMATIONS	Allusions; hints
INTRACTABLY	Inflexibly; in a headstrong manner
IRRESOLUTE	Uncertain; hesitant
JOVIAL	Jolly; happy
LAMENTS	Moans; wails
MANIPULATES	Maneuvers; moves

MOROSELY	Gloomily; sullenly
NETTLED	Bothered; peeved
NONPLUSED	Bewildered; puzzled
OBSTINATE	Stubborn; headstrong
OCULIST	Eye doctor
OMINOUSLY	Threateningly; darkly; gloomily

PANTOMIME	Gestures without voice
PAROXYSM	Fit; attack
PLACATING	Satisfying; gratifying
PLAINTIVELY	Sorrowfully; sadly
PRIMER	Manual; handbook
PROFFERED	Offered forth

PUMMELS	Thrashes; beats
RECOMMENCED	Repeated; began again
RELINQUISHES	Resigns; gives up
REPROACHFULLY	Disapprovingly; critically
RESOLUTELY	Deliberately; willfully
SOLICITUDE	Concern

SPINSTER	Old, unmarried woman
SWADDLED	Wrapped up
TEMPERANCE	Moderation
TRACHOMA	Inflammation of the eyelids
TRANSFIXED	Motionless; frozen
TREPIDATION	Fear; alarm

TYRANT	Harsh, cruel leader
UNAVAILING	Hopeless; futile
UNKEMPT	Disorderly; messy
UNOBSTRUCTED	In open view
UNPERTURBED	Undisturbed; unbothered
VALIANTLY	Bravely; courageously

VEXEDLY	Irritatedly
VIGIL	A watch
VIVACIOUS	Lively; spirited
VOLUMINOUS	Bulky; large
WITHERING	Shrinking
WOEBEGONE	Miserable; sorrowful

WRITHES	Twists from pain; flails

Miracle Worker Vocabulary

WRITHES	REPROACHFULLY	AFFLICTION	DESICCATED	UNKEMPT
DIMINUTIVE	EMPHATIC	CONSPICUOUSLY	COMPELLED	FRIVOLOUS
NONPLUSED	TYRANT	FREE SPACE	FACETIOUSLY	UNPERTURBED
DISHEVELED	MANIPULATES	RELINQUISHES	INTERPOSES	PLACATING
VALIANTLY	SPINSTER	PANTOMIME	DOURLY	VIGIL

Miracle Worker Vocabulary

SOLICITUDE	INARTICULATE	INTIMATIONS	PROFFERED	TRACHOMA
INTERMINABLE	CONSUMMATELY	AMIABLY	RESOLUTELY	ASPERITY
DEPRIVATION	PLAINTIVELY	FREE SPACE	UNAVAILING	WITHERING
TRANSFIXED	WOEBEGONE	IMPERCEPTIBLY	TEMPERANCE	NETTLED
PRIMER	FORLORN	DEVOUTNESS	OCULIST	INDOLENT

Miracle Worker Vocabulary

WOEBEGONE	AVERSION	DISENGAGE	FACETIOUSLY	UNKEMPT
IMPERCEPTIBLY	PAROXYSM	SOLICITUDE	VEXEDLY	UNAVAILING
WITHERING	TYRANT	FREE SPACE	DEPRIVATION	WRITHES
INARTICULATE	ALMSHOUSE	INTRACTABLY	CONSPICUOUSLY	INEXORABLY
DEVOUTNESS	APPRAISAL	CONSUMMATELY	BAFFLED	CHIVALROUS

Miracle Worker Vocabulary

DOURLY	INDOLENT	PUMMELS	AMIABLY	RECOMMENCED
IRRESOLUTE	VOLUMINOUS	CARICATURE	PLACATING	TEMPERANCE
LAMENTS	SPINSTER	FREE SPACE	OBSTINATE	NONPLUSED
TREPIDATION	JOVIAL	COMPUNCTION	AFFLICTION	INTERMINABLE
DEFERENTIAL	EMPHATIC	PRIMER	IMPERTINENT	TRANSFIXED

Miracle Worker Vocabulary

PANTOMIME	INTERMINABLE	DESICCATED	TEMPERANCE	INTIMATIONS
BAFFLED	OMINOUSLY	UNPERTURBED	BENIGN	PROFFERED
WITHERING	DEFERENTIAL	FREE SPACE	CONSUMMATELY	MANIPULATES
DIMINUTIVE	RECOMMENCED	DEVOUTNESS	DOURLY	OCULIST
PAROXYSM	RELINQUISHES	PLAINTIVELY	VALIANTLY	PRIMER

Miracle Worker Vocabulary

WRITHES	APPRAISAL	INARTICULATE	INEFFECTUAL	AMIABLY
EMPHATIC	REPROACHFULLY	OBSTINATE	SOLICITUDE	TREPIDATION
INEXORABLY	ASPERITY	FREE SPACE	COMPELLED	VIGIL
VEXEDLY	DISHEVELED	DEPRIVATION	HAGGARD	INDIGNANTLY
DISENGAGE	PUMMELS	FACETIOUSLY	AVERSION	COMPUNCTION

Miracle Worker Vocabulary

ASPERITY	COMPELLED	INDIGNANTLY	TREPIDATION	DISHEVELED
BENIGN	CHIVALROUS	AFFLICTION	UNAVAILING	VIGIL
FACETIOUSLY	BAFFLED	FREE SPACE	INTERPOSES	INEFFECTUAL
INTERMINABLE	CONSPICUOUSLY	TRANSFIXED	SWADDLED	OMINOUSLY
UNOBSTRUCTED	PLACATING	FORLORN	WITHERING	PROFFERED

Miracle Worker Vocabulary

PLAINTIVELY	ALMSHOUSE	NETTLED	INTRACTABLY	IMPERCEPTIBLY
IMPERIOUS	DEVOUTNESS	OCULIST	OBSTINATE	TRACHOMA
FRIVOLOUS	NONPLUSED	FREE SPACE	UNKEMPT	VIVACIOUS
AMIABLY	DESICCATED	IRRESOLUTE	BLANDLY	INTIMATIONS
INDOLENT	IMPERTINENT	RELINQUISHES	TEMPERANCE	INARTICULATE

Miracle Worker Vocabulary

CONSPICUOUSLY	FRIVOLOUS	SPINSTER	IMPERCEPTIBLY	WITHERING
DISENGAGE	TYRANT	VIVACIOUS	PAROXYSM	RECOMMENCED
AFFLICTION	PRIMER	FREE SPACE	DESICCATED	UNKEMPT
NONPLUSED	EMPHATIC	BENIGN	INTERMINABLE	DEVOUTNESS
INARTICULATE	TREPIDATION	PLAINTIVELY	AMIABLY	WOEBEGONE

Miracle Worker Vocabulary

CARICATURE	VIGIL	MOROSELY	PROFFERED	TEMPERANCE
OBSTINATE	REPROACHFULLY	INDOLENT	LAMENTS	UNAVAILING
IMPUDENCE	OCULIST	FREE SPACE	INDIGNANTLY	PUMMELS
APPRAISAL	ALMSHOUSE	DIMINUTIVE	ASPERITY	DISHEVELED
FORLORN	INTRACTABLY	MANIPULATES	INEXORABLY	BAFFLED

Miracle Worker Vocabulary

APPARAISAL	FRIVOLOUS	IRRESOLUTE	INTRACTABLY	DISHEVELED
IMPUDENCE	INTERPOSES	WOEBEGONE	IMPERIOUS	IMPASSIVELY
INDULGENT	CONSPICUOUSLY	FREE SPACE	BAFFLED	DEPRIVATION
UNKEMPT	UNPERTURBED	PANTOMIME	EMPHATIC	NETTLED
ASPERITY	WRITHES	INDOLENT	OBSTINATE	JOVIAL

Miracle Worker Vocabulary

FACETIOUSLY	TRANSFIXED	COMBATIVE	CHIVALROUS	DIMINUTIVE
PLAINTIVELY	VIGIL	MOROSELY	CONSUMMATELY	VEXEDLY
RELINQUISHES	PUMMELS	FREE SPACE	BENIGN	UNOBSTRUCTED
PLACATING	RESOLUTELY	HAGGARD	INDIGNANTLY	DEVOUTNESS
TEMPERANCE	AMIABLY	DEFERENTIAL	INARTICULATE	MANIPULATES

Miracle Worker Vocabulary

VOLUMINOUS	AMIABLY	INARTICULATE	INEFFECTUAL	PRIMER
DESICCATED	TREPIDATION	SOLICITUDE	VIVACIOUS	FORLORN
EMPHATIC	APPRAISAL	FREE SPACE	REPROACHFULLY	AVERSION
WITHERING	OMINOUSLY	RECOMMENCED	INDOLENT	PLACATING
CONSPICUOUSLY	ASPERITY	INTRACTABLY	RESOLUTELY	DISHEVELED

Miracle Worker Vocabulary

AFFLICTION	CHIVALROUS	DEPRIVATION	TEMPERANCE	HAGGARD
INEXORABLY	NETTLED	DISENGAGE	PAROXYSM	MOROSELY
CARICATURE	BAFFLED	FREE SPACE	OBSTINATE	DEVOUTNESS
TRACHOMA	LAMENTS	IMPERTINENT	PANTOMIME	OCULIST
IMPERIOUS	TRANSFIXED	COMBATIVE	INDIGNANTLY	NONPLUSED

Miracle Worker Vocabulary

TREPIDATION	RELINQUISHES	LAMENTS	DESICCATED	VOLUMINOUS
FORLORN	BENIGN	RECOMMENCED	PROFFERED	VEXEDLY
WRITHES	BLANDLY	FREE SPACE	JOVIAL	IMPUDENCE
REPROACHFULLY	AVERSION	INEXORABLY	DISENGAGE	PRIMER
SWADDLED	OBSTINATE	WITHERING	TYRANT	PLACATING

Miracle Worker Vocabulary

INDOLENT	IMPERCEPTIBLY	TRANSFIXED	TEMPERANCE	RESOLUTELY
WOEBEGONE	CHIVALROUS	SPINSTER	BAFFLED	CONSPICUOUSLY
DOURLY	COMBATIVE	FREE SPACE	VIVACIOUS	VIGIL
INTERMINABLE	INEFFECTUAL	MOROSELY	INTRACTABLY	DIMINUTIVE
CARICATURE	CONSUMMATELY	PANTOMIME	DISHEVELED	AMIABLY

Miracle Worker Vocabulary

INTIMATIONS	DIMINUTIVE	EMPHATIC	CARICATURE	DEFERENTIAL
UNAVAILING	PROFFERED	PRIMER	OBSTINATE	FORLORN
AFFLICTION	ALMSHOUSE	FREE SPACE	WOEBEGONE	TRANSFIXED
NETTLED	RESOLUTELY	WITHERING	DEPRIVATION	INTRACTABLY
TEMPERANCE	TREPIDATION	UNPERTURBED	BENIGN	FACETIOUSLY

Miracle Worker Vocabulary

FRIVOLOUS	DISHEVELED	INEFFECTUAL	CONSUMMATELY	INTERPOSES
COMBATIVE	VEXEDLY	TYRANT	INDOLENT	VALIANTLY
NONPLUSED	LAMENTS	FREE SPACE	UNKEMPT	IMPERCEPTIBLY
CONSPICUOUSLY	SWADDLED	ASPERITY	COMPUNCTION	DEVOUTNESS
REPROACHFULLY	INDULGENT	WRITHES	RELINQUISHES	MOROSELY

Miracle Worker Vocabulary

OMINOUSLY	IMPASSIVELY	AVERSION	DOURLY	HAGGARD
LAMENTS	UNKEMPT	IMPERCEPTIBLY	AFFLICTION	COMPUNCTION
DISENGAGE	TREPIDATION	FREE SPACE	FRIVOLOUS	OCULIST
REPROACHFULLY	INEFFECTUAL	SWADDLED	RECOMMENCED	CONSPICUOUSLY
NONPLUSED	IRRESOLUTE	PAROXYSM	INTERMINABLE	DEVOUTNESS

Miracle Worker Vocabulary

UNOBSTRUCTED	VIGIL	VALIANTLY	BENIGN	PRIMER
FORLORN	INDULGENT	WOEBEGONE	DEFERENTIAL	PLAINTIVELY
CHIVALROUS	UNAVAILING	FREE SPACE	DIMINUTIVE	INDIGNANTLY
IMPERIOUS	DEPRIVATION	TRANSFIXED	SOLICITUDE	FACETIOUSLY
VIVACIOUS	PLACATING	TYRANT	WRITHES	ASPERITY

Miracle Worker Vocabulary

IMPERIOUS	APPRAISAL	WITHERING	RECOMMENCED	CONSPICUOUSLY
COMPUNCTION	RELINQUISHES	DISENGAGE	DEPRIVATION	TRACHOMA
WOEBEGONE	REPROACHFULLY	FREE SPACE	DIMINUTIVE	DOURLY
NONPLUSED	PRIMER	ASPERITY	INARTICULATE	CONSUMMATELY
VIVACIOUS	VOLUMINOUS	INDOLENT	OBSTINATE	JOVIAL

Miracle Worker Vocabulary

NETTLED	UNKEMPT	FACETIOUSLY	PROFFERED	INTIMATIONS
INTERPOSES	DEVOUTNESS	PANTOMIME	INEFFECTUAL	IMPERCEPTIBLY
WRITHES	AVERSION	FREE SPACE	PUMMELS	EMPHATIC
ALMSHOUSE	IMPASSIVELY	PAROXYSM	TREPIDATION	CARICATURE
COMPELLED	DEFERENTIAL	TRANSFIXED	IMPUDENCE	COMBATIVE

Miracle Worker Vocabulary

DISENGAGE	PUMMELS	RECOMMENCED	LAMENTS	ASPERITY
INDOLENT	TRANSFIXED	VEXEDLY	IRRESOLUTE	REPROACHFULLY
NETTLED	PLAINTIVELY	FREE SPACE	OMINOUSLY	INARTICULATE
IMPERCEPTIBLY	APPRAISAL	TYRANT	EMPHATIC	FORLORN
COMPUNCTION	SWADDLED	IMPERIOUS	CARICATURE	PLACATING

Miracle Worker Vocabulary

PROFFERED	CONSUMMATELY	AVERSION	INTRACTABLY	TREPIDATION
TRACHOMA	VOLUMINOUS	PAROXYSM	INEXORABLY	DESICCATED
VIGIL	UNAVAILING	FREE SPACE	INEFFECTUAL	INDULGENT
COMBATIVE	INTIMATIONS	INDIGNANTLY	ALMSHOUSE	CHIVALROUS
MANIPULATES	BLANDLY	BAFFLED	UNKEMPT	NONPLUSED

Miracle Worker Vocabulary

TRANSFIXED	COMPUNCTION	IMPUDENCE	SWADDLED	CHIVALROUS
NONPLUSED	LAMENTS	UNOBSTRUCTED	NETTLED	INTERPOSES
TRACHOMA	IMPERIOUS	FREE SPACE	INTRACTABLY	UNAVAILING
FRIVOLOUS	DISENGAGE	SPINSTER	IMPERCEPTIBLY	CONSPICUOUSLY
DESICCATED	IMPASSIVELY	INEFFECTUAL	VIGIL	IRRESOLUTE

Miracle Worker Vocabulary

IMPERTINENT	DEVOUTNESS	INDULGENT	DEPRIVATION	INTIMATIONS
PUMMELS	BLANDLY	INDOLENT	EMPHATIC	AFFLICTION
RECOMMENCED	VIVACIOUS	FREE SPACE	VALIANTLY	COMPELLED
UNPERTURBED	TYRANT	RESOLUTELY	WOEBEGONE	VOLUMINOUS
PRIMER	DIMINUTIVE	OCULIST	AVERSION	BAFFLED

Miracle Worker Vocabulary

DISHEVELED	PROFFERED	INDULGENT	INTERMINABLE	WITHERING
SWADDLED	COMPELLED	IMPERIOUS	INEXORABLY	REPROACHFULLY
LAMENTS	COMBATIVE	FREE SPACE	MANIPULATES	TRACHOMA
COMPUNCTION	DOURLY	RESOLUTELY	INDOLENT	INTIMATIONS
MOROSELY	OBSTINATE	VIGIL	AMIABLY	PRIMER

Miracle Worker Vocabulary

IMPERTINENT	RECOMMENCED	HAGGARD	PUMMELS	PAROXYSM
CHIVALROUS	ASPERITY	DEFERENTIAL	WOEBEGONE	INTRACTABLY
DEVOUTNESS	INARTICULATE	FREE SPACE	IMPASSIVELY	TYRANT
ALMSHOUSE	TREPIDATION	SOLICITUDE	TRANSFIXED	BAFFLED
PLACATING	APPRAISAL	BLANDLY	VIVACIOUS	AVERSION

Miracle Worker Vocabulary

MOROSELY	INEFFECTUAL	DIMINUTIVE	BENIGN	TRACHOMA
ASPERITY	OBSTINATE	PAROXYSM	AVERSION	CONSPICUOUSLY
FORLORN	PLACATING	FREE SPACE	INDOLENT	IMPERTINENT
UNOBSTRUCTED	WITHERING	REPROACHFULLY	VIGIL	NONPLUSED
ALMSHOUSE	RESOLUTELY	SWADDLED	IRRESOLUTE	COMPELLED

Miracle Worker Vocabulary

HAGGARD	IMPASSIVELY	CONSUMMATELY	WOEBEGONE	UNPERTURBED
INTIMATIONS	TREPIDATION	DEFERENTIAL	OMINOUSLY	BAFFLED
DESICCATED	NETTLED	FREE SPACE	VEXEDLY	INDULGENT
INARTICULATE	VALIANTLY	AMIABLY	PLAINTIVELY	DOURLY
LAMENTS	DEVOUTNESS	IMPUDENCE	COMBATIVE	VOLUMINOUS

Miracle Worker Vocabulary

UNAVAILING	RECOMMENCED	BLANDLY	SWADDLED	PANTOMIME
ALMSHOUSE	INTIMATIONS	COMPUNCTION	UNOBSTRUCTED	FACETIOUSLY
TYRANT	WITHERING	FREE SPACE	INEFFECTUAL	BAFFLED
SPINSTER	WRITHES	INTERMINABLE	PAROXYSM	VIGIL
OCULIST	REPROACHFULLY	CONSPICUOUSLY	SOLICITUDE	DEVOUTNESS

Miracle Worker Vocabulary

INTRACTABLY	EMPHATIC	BENIGN	FORLORN	PROFFERED
AFFLICTION	AVERSION	JOVIAL	IMPUDENCE	VALIANTLY
WOEBEGONE	INDIGNANTLY	FREE SPACE	CONSUMMATELY	RESOLUTELY
COMBATIVE	DOURLY	TREPIDATION	PUMMELS	PLACATING
DISENGAGE	OBSTINATE	DEFERENTIAL	TRANSFIXED	DESICCATED

www.ingramcontent.com/pod-product-compliance
Lightning Source LLC
Chambersburg PA
CBHW081452070526
44586CB00019B/2317